Printed in France for Floraprint Ltd., Nottingham.
The publisher wishes to thank
Adrian Bloom of Blooms Nurseries Ltd,
for valuable technical help
and Michael Warren and Harry Smith
for outstanding photography.

Alan Bloom is probably better qualified than any other person to write about Hardy Perennials. Since 1930 when he started his own business, his nursery has become the largest of its kind in Europe. In 1946 he moved his nursery from Oakington, Cambridge to its present home at Bressingham near Diss in Norfolk, and it is there that is situated one of the most comprehensive collections of Perennials in the world. The 'Dell Garden' as it is called was laid out by Alan Bloom himself and now covers over 5 acres and 5 000 species and varieties of Hardy Perennials. These include not only hundreds of uncommon species but several varieties raised at Bressingham and introduced to the public.

The many books and articles written by Alan Bloom reflect the wealth of experience he has gained in trying to make the best use of Hardy Perennials, and this book brings you the opportunity to share beauty he has created at Bressingham.

Cover :
This was known as The Dell before the author went to live at Bressingham and though its possibilities as a garden were seen, it was over 10 years before it could be converted from meadow. Beds were dug out and with many variations in aspect, shade and moisture loving plants were so successfully grown that eventually the gardens took up a total of 5 acres.

HARDY PERENNIALS
for the garden

What are Hardy Perennials?

There are some wrong ideas in circulation as to what Hardy Perennials are. To some they are known as, 'Herbaceous Border Plants' but 'Hardy Perennials' is the better term because is conveys most—once it is fully understood. By dividing the two words we can arrive at its full and true meaning. A hardy plant—as distinct from a shrub, bush or tree, is one that will withstand winter frost and damp. It has to be relied upon to do this in our climate as it is expected to re-appear after the winter is over and flower again year after year. Perennial means just that, a plant that re-appears year after year as opposed to an annual which only flowers once and dies. Not all Hardy Perennials are truly herbaceous because the latter term means that foliage dies down in autumn and new growth is made in spring, but some keep their foliage throughout the winter.

The quest for variety.

The range of such plants which are both hardy and perennial is immense. It is far wider than most people imagine, who only grow such things as Lupins, Delphiniums, Michaelmas Daisies and a few others. This book is designed to show not only the best of subjects already popular, but to illustrate something of the rich variety of less common kinds in existence and available from specialist nurseries. In this respect it will undoubtedly fill a need, because variety makes for continuity in the garden, as well as pleasing changes in form and colours from the more ordinary kinds. To widen the variety one grows and can rely upon, is for all keen gardeners a very stimulating process. To enhance one's range is to create new interests, to widen one's knowledge and to achieve a hitherto unsuspected joy and satisfaction by way of reward for one's efforts.

Adaptability.

But the criterion is garden worthiness, coupled with reliability. Difficult or unreliable subjects are not included in this book. All plants possess a measure of adaptability in regard to soil, situation and climate, and it must be understood that no plant can possibly be adaptable to every condition. For this reason every subject recommended is described with this in mind and though the majority are adaptable to most conditions they are likely to encounter, any special needs are mentioned for those with a limited range of adaptability.

Garden worthiness.

The reliability factor must take account not only of hardiness and longevity, though these must be of paramount importance. Garden merit must also be reckoned with on such matters as a long flowering period, of form and grace as well as the display it gives, and the question of whether or not it will stand without supports.

To have to stake or support, is a chore that no one could be blamed for shirking unless they are specially fond of such kinds as Delphiniums which scarcely ever can stand unaided.

An Island Bed and a weeping willow with older trees behind, offered the site for a thatched shelter or summer house, which Alan Bloom built in 1960 using colourful Norfolk flint stones.

Natural conditions for growth.

Ease of maintenance, is a vital point, and it must be said that a good many conventional herbaceous borders exist which are anything but easy to maintain. This is almost invariably due to too many plants being crammed into too narrow a space. The old idea—when labour was cheap—was to make a massed planting in an artificially created border, with a wall or hedge as backing. This is the conventional herbaceous border, and it is small wonder that nowadays they are regarded as troublesome to maintain. The reason is that with over close planting, the effect of the backing is to make the growth drawn and spindly. Lack of light and the free circulation of air during the growing period produces taller, weaker stems.

The narrower the border in relation to the height of the backing or the type of plants grown—often too tall growing anyway—the more artificial, incongruous and troublesome it is.

Making a careful choice.

It is however realised that in some gardens, where space is restricted, the usual rectangular garden area seems to lend itself to a border of some kind against the boundary hedge or fence and a lawn in the centre. In cases where no change from such a pattern can be considered, there are ways and means of making a comparatively trouble free border so long as a careful choice of plants is made. This is very important, whether or not they are used in company with shrubs, for it should be noted here that many kinds of perennials are very complementary to shrubs. Their range is so great that some can be used as ground coverers, whilst others can provide colour and interest after the majority of shrubs have finished flowering.

Key to success

This, along with other uses to which Hardy Perennials can be put, is dealt with further on, but here the best way of growing them in variety for their own sakes must be more fully covered. Undoubtedly the best means is that of growing them In Island Beds as distinct from the conventional one sided affair with a backing wall, hedge or fence. An Island Bed is closer to natural conditions, allowing free circulation of strength giving air and for all but shade lovers, the benefit of light.

The majority of Perennials prefer an open situation—open to sun, light and air, and by making a careful selection of subjects, one

A broad grass path, slightly sunken was made so as to break up the natural flatness of the meadow at Bressingham, to leave sloping beds on either side. The one on the right is planted with alpines and dwarf shrubs.

can achieve variety in form, height and colour from early spring to late autumn, with practically no staking and the minimum of labour generally.

Island beds.

Island Beds can not only be seen from all sides, but access to them for such necessary maintenance tasks as hoeing or weeding is much easier than with the old conventional border style.
With light and air plants grow to the height nature intended and no more.   This brings them into
the most effective position from the display point of view and creates fewer problems when some
kinds need replanting, as some do every few years, to keep them vigorous and free flowering.
All this however depends on one other important factor—that of spacing and the preference it
suggests of growing different kinds in groups.   So often the effect is spoiled by dotting a plant
here and there indiscriminately even to the extent of duplication.

*Roof top view of the first experimental Island Beds at Bressingham, carved out from a neglected lawn,
in 1952-1953.*

Common sense planning.

Naturally an Island Bed should have its tallest growing subjects near the centre, whereas of course in a one-sided border they must be placed at the rear. This grading of heights is purely for effect, so that each kind can be seen and appreciated. Given adequate width this is easy to arrange so long as one remembers or knows the height to which each kind can be expected to grow.

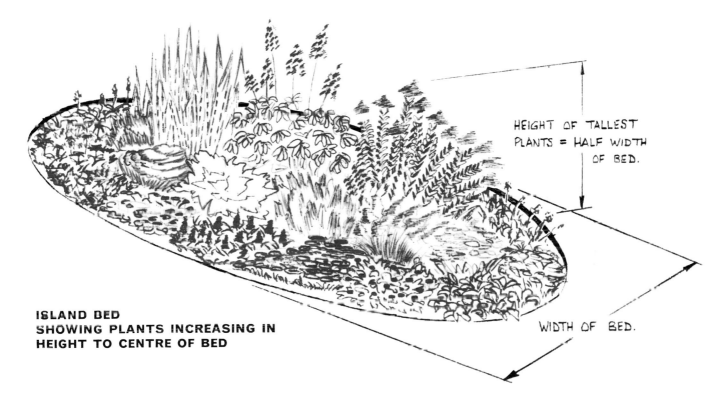

HEIGHT OF TALLEST PLANTS = HALF WIDTH OF BED.

WIDTH OF BED.

**ISLAND BED
SHOWING PLANTS INCREASING IN
HEIGHT TO CENTRE OF BED**

Such details are included in the description of each kind illustrated, and most specialists catalogues provide them. In selecting a variety restrict the height according to the width of the border. The narrower it is, the shorter should be the tallest kinds chosen. A useful rule to follow is to divide by two the width of the border, in feet, and to keep within the limit this gives in regard to height. A border of any type, of say 8 feet wide, should contain nothing taller than about four feet. Narrow beds or borders and excessively tall plants simply do not make sense. But they make for trouble and loss in terms of effectiveness of display.

It can be assumed that a reader wishing to go in for perennials will chose one or more of three courses. A new garden will call for a decision as to where a bed or border should be. The site may be clear for an Island Bed, and it would be a commendable decision to use a plot nearer the centre, rather than a strip along the boundary. The latter would be much better as a screening border for shrubs, interplanted with ground coverers, leaving the centre for both lawn and an Island Bed if the latter appeals. It need not of course, occupy the exact centre. Most garden plots are oblong, and an Island Bed could well be placed towards one end, as a break say, between the kitchen and ornamental sections. In such a case, viewed as it would be mainly from the house, the grading of heights should be more gradual from this aspect than from the rear.

At the back some access should be given by a path, however narrow, and beside this could be planted groups of early flowering perennials such as Primroses, Pulmonarias, etc. These would be over by the time the summer perennials grew tall enough to hide them.

SEM-ISLAND BED SHOWING BUILD-UP OF PLANTS MAINLY FROM THE FRONT

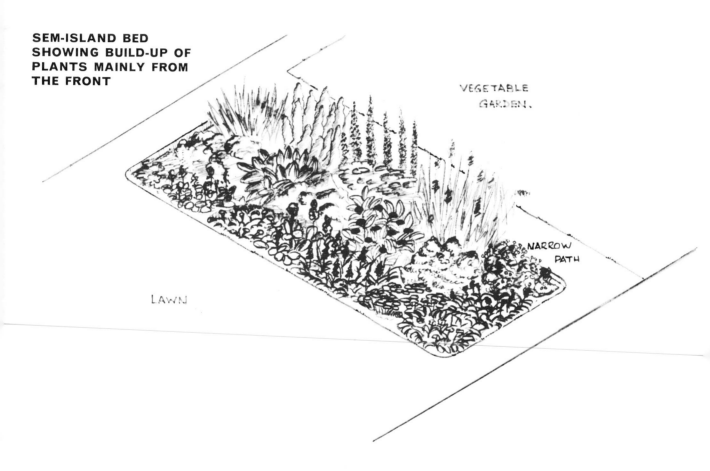

Grading heights.

This design could be termed as a semi-island bed, distinct from the true type, which aims to have a more or less even grading of heights from every angle, as one walks around its perimeter. Bearing in mind the need to restrict heights when making a selection according to the width of the bed, with the tallest in the centre part, the effect is very pleasing. One should also try to intersperse kinds having differing habits of growth, so as to break up any tendency to flatness or regimentation. Some kinds, especially those of the Daisy family have flowers more or less on one level. Others are spikey in growth—like Lupins and Kniphofias. It is by planting the latter in groups amongst the former that the best possible effect is achieved—with an eye to continuity as well.

SEMI-ISLAND BED PLANTING DIAGRAM

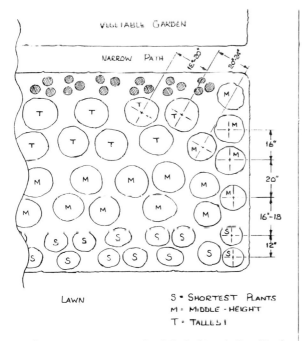

NOTE THE LATE WINTER - EARLY SPRING FLOWERING
ITEMS THUS ⬤ AT BACK OF BED.

Spacing for effect.

Spacing, as will be seen, is also important. Assuming groups of three or more plants are used of one kind, rather more space should be allowed around each group than between each plant comprising the group. The average planting space is 16''-18'' from plant to plant, but between groups it should be 20''-22''.

The more robust growing kinds would of course need wider spacing, but for dwarfer, slower growing subjects it can be less.

Avoiding trouble.

It follows too, that if a vigorous, tall or very robust kind is planted next to another with much slower or lowly growth the latter will suffer after the first season or two. Segregation is easy to practice. It means simply, that in selecting and placing, growth rate as well as height should be taken into account, so as to keep the vigorous kinds more or less together in one part of the bed or border and the slow spreaders in another. Mention of this should not however, be taken as a deterrent to readers. None of the subjects mentioned in this book are of weedy nature, and those that are merely vigorous can easily be curbed should their spread become excessive.

PLANTING DIAGRAM OF AN ISLAND BED
SHOWN WITH THE MINIMUM SUGGESTED GROUPING OF THREE PLANTS PER KIND

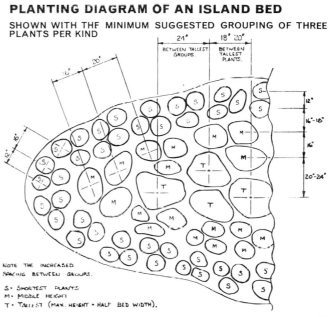

NOTE THE INCREASED
SPACING BETWEEN GROUPS.

S - SHORTEST PLANTS
M - MIDDLE HEIGHT
T - TALLEST (MAX. HEIGHT = HALF BED WIDTH).

Continuity and display.

Continuity is also a matter of making a right selection. Not many kinds flower before May, and the peak period for Hardy Perennials is from mid June to late August. There exists sufficient variety to have the maximum display in spring, summer or autumn, but most people prefer to have them cover as long a period as possible. This may mean placing more than ordinary emphasis on the very early and very late flowering kinds if fairly regular continuity is to be achieved. In my own garden, where a very wide variety exists, the first flowers appear in February, and in mild winters, there are still flowers to be seen the following Christmas.
A careful selection can also achieve a predominance of favourite colours or colour combinations. Sufficient variety exists to do this, as well as to use the many grey, silvery and variegated foliage plants if any of these hold a special appeal.

FIRST REQUISITES.

Weeds.

The sensible approach to any form of gardening is to decide first whether the piece of ground you have is suitable for the type of decorative plants you wish to grow. All plants have their limits of adaptability, and whilst Hardy Perennials are generally very adaptable, it is best to make sure that the soil and situation are suitable, if for instance a wide variety is intended. The soil does not need to be specially rich. What is most important is that it should be free of harmful perennial weeds, such as couch grass, ground elder, creeping thistle, marestail and creeping cress. Annual weeds, like groundsel, chickweed etc, matter much less because they are easily destroyed, but it would be asking for trouble to plant a bed or border already infested with perennial weeds.

Drainage.

Drainage is another essential. One cannot expect plants to flourish in soil that is wet and sticky over winter. Often such soils dry out in summer and bake hard in the sun. Plants need moisture only during their growing period between spring and autumn, and more plants die from excessive winter wet, when they are dormant, than in the driest of summers.

Heavy clay soils are the most difficult to cultivate, but they can be greatly improved by under-draining with pipes, coarse gravel, brickbats, laid in trenches about 2 feet deep and about 6 inches wide. Clay soil can also be improved by adding peat or sand mixed in when digging, but winter sogginess can only be overcome by drainage, with an outlet to a ditch or sump.

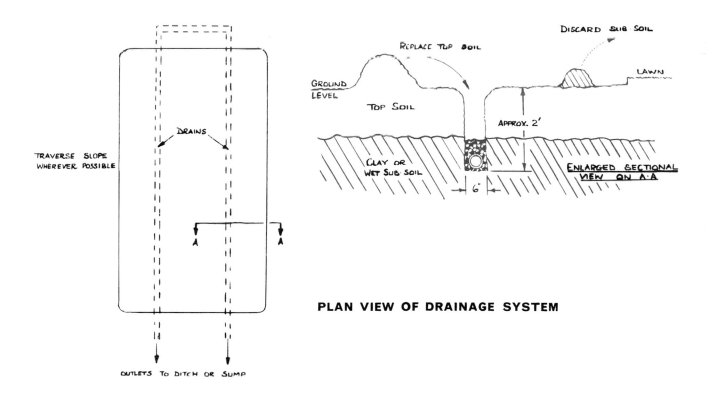

PLAN VIEW OF DRAINAGE SYSTEM

Soils.

Sandy or gravelly soils are almost always free draining. Because of this they are likely to dry out most in summer and are most likely to respond to enrichment with manure, compost or peat. If peat alone is used, some organic fertiliser should be used In conjunction with it. Peat is also ideal for chalky soils which not only lack humus but have excessive alkalinity. Some plants dislike lime, and though the majority of kinds are lime tolerant, it is worth the little trouble it takes, if in doubt, to have a lime test taken before investing in plants which dislike alkalinity.

A neutral soil in this respect, with a 6.0 to 7.0 PH is ideal, because one can then grow almost anything.

Shade and moisture are less important factors. Moisture can usually be added by overhead watering, or from the overflow of a pool, if one wishes to grow moisture loving plants.

Shade is less easy to contrive if no natural shade in a garden exists, though usually a wall, if not a tree, will be found to lessen harmful sunlight to shade loving plants. Some of the most choice and beautiful plants are happy only in shade where there is no real lack of moisture for long. These are natives of dampish woods, where dappled or broken shade comes from tall trees, and it should be said that not many kinds prefer the deep shade of close planted evergreens.

The most difficult of all places to fill with a wide variety of Hardy Perennials, Is dry shade, where low overhanging branches keep off the rain and where tree roots have first call on any existing moisture. Only a score or so of kinds exists that will tolerate such inhospitable conditions, yet in many gardens, such spots can be filled with trouble free ground coverers, if only their owners knew about them.

Ground coverers.

Ground covering perennials also have their uses amongst shrubs, as well as for those with problematical banks, verges etc. The sunnier the position, the wider the selection becomes available to fill them, and the demand for ground covering plants these days indicates the need some people have of filling up garden space so as to reduce maintenance to the absolute minimum. There are all kinds of gardeners, just as there are all kinds of gardens and plants with which to fill them. But without any doubt, the greatest rewards in gardening come to those who are prepared to take some trouble in growing as well as possible the widest range of plants their garden will support. Given a common sense approach, one can expect not only a return comparable with the effort, but a bonus as well in terms of interest and satisfaction.

Rewards.

Haphazard gardeners seldom achieve much. One needs to be much more deliberate, to scheme and acquire knowledge well in advance, before embarking on any new project. Such knowledge will of itself create new interests, as well as to avoid the pitfalls of ignorance. The aim should therefore be to plan within the limitations imposed by space, soil, climate and environmental situations, and then to select the kinds of plants which one can be reasonably sure will succeed under these conditions. This book is designed to help in various ways those who for lack of

In the foreground it is both shady and dry. Spring flowers flourish along with drought resistant ground coverers.

knowledge have either failed or been afraid to begin, as well as those who having begun, wish to raise their sights a little higher to the wealth of variety in beautiful, easy to grow plants which they scarcely knew existed.

Improving an old border.

A decision with which some may be faced is how to improve an old existing 'Herbaceous Border' of the conventional one-sided type.

It may have become a nuisance if not an eyesore because it is too narrow in relation to the tall, rank growing kinds it still contains. One should be pretty ruthless and treat the worst offenders (which have probably choked or over-run choicer, more worthy kinds) as if they were weeds. Along with any other weeds the old border may harbour, destroy all unwanted plants, dig over thoroughly and make a completely new beginning.

If the border is capable of being widened, even if this means taking in a strip of lawn, it will be worth the sacrifice. It would be no sacrifice at all to dig up a gravel path or old box edging, for the former is usually superfluous and the latter a harbour for slugs and snails. When it comes to replanting, having made a selection of worth while subjects, allow sufficient space at the rear for access and avoid the baneful effect a hedge so often has, bearing in mind that light and air are as necessary to strong reliable growth, as are moisture and sustenance.

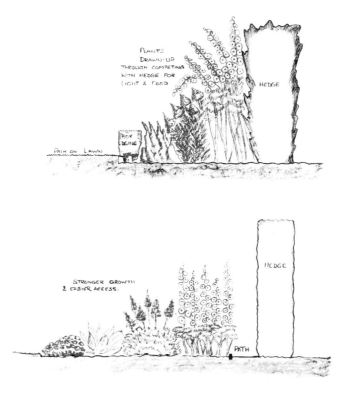

Awkward spots.

Another possible decision is whether or not to use a given site or space, which is simply in need of filling. Such a space may be damp, shady or a dry impoverished slope. With all the variations there could be, on the score of soil and situation, it is impossible to make specific recommendations.

What matters most is to assess potentialities as well as the drawbacks of a given site, and be extra careful to make a selection which will grow there. This comes back to one of the guiding principles mentioned earlier—of choosing subjects most likely to succeed or adapt themselves to the prevailing circumstances. It is not so difficult as one might at first imagine, and this book provides recommended lists for a variety of situations.

Planning.

A little more needs to be said about planning. This book gives one or two diagrams on the layout of both an Island Bed and Conventional Border. Some catalogues offer a free plan, with a price for the collection of plants it will hold. But such sterotyped plans can scarcely be applicable to every variation there could be in regard to soil and situation, and wherever possible it is preferable to do one's own planning. It is not difficult and in the process one can learn a great deal of vital knowledge. The only need is for a sheet of graph paper and having chosen a site, translate its outline to a scale that will suit.

It is simply a matter of filling in the names of the plants you have selected, in their appropriate places, on the lines of the examples given on p. 13. Having done so and having prepared the site, place marker sticks or labels (numbered if the names are too difficult), so that when planting times comes, they can be laid out and planted precisely as planned. If an error regarding placing occurs it will show up when flowering time comes, and in the following autumn or spring the necessary switch can safely be made. The guiding principles given in regard to preparation, planning and planting are applicable to any type of border or bed.

They also apply to shapes and sizes of beds and here it should be said that personal preferences can be given a large measure of freedom. If a geometric design, whether severely oblong or a free form border appeals then the choice is yours. The one-sided border has been the conventional shape, and if the garden lends itself only to this type, it would be wiser not to go in for a very irregular curving frontage to it. The Island Bed offers much more scope, and if any informal outlines exist already in the garden, then it is an easy matter to make a free form bed in keeping with a tree, shrubbery or any other feature. An Island Bed set in a rectangular lawn would however appear somewhat incongruous if it were not in keeping by having it of some free form irregular shape. In these circumstances an inner rectangle for the bed, or for that matter an oval or circular shape would fit in perfectly well.

The question of the size of the bed will depend almost entirely on the size of the garden, if not on the size or colour of one's bank balance. In either case a midget border could be the solution. Perennials are so adaptable that a bed or border of no more than eight square yards, could be made to hold a very pleasing variety of plants. If one were restricted to thirty or forty plants, one of a kind, it would at least be a beginning.

Bearing in mind that even some so-called Rock Plants are but dwarf hardy perennials it is easy enough to make a selection to suit the size of the bed. The important thing is to restrict that selection, so far as heights are concerned, to suit the site—to avoid having kinds that grow too tall for the width of the bed or border. A midget bed or border of say 5 feet wide, should not contain anything more than about 2 ½ feet tall. There are hosts of beautiful plants that grow below that height. The only kinds one should avoid are the true Alpines which hug the ground, but for such small beds there is no lack of variety of Dwarf Perennials flowering at heights of about 6 inches upwards.

PHLOX PRINCE OF ORANGE	SALVIA SUPERBA	ACHILLEA GOLD PLATE	MACLEAYA CORDIFOLIA	DELPHINIUM BLUE	ASTER HARRINGTONS PINK	LUPIN YELLOW	VERONICA VIRGINICA ALBA
ASTER CRIMSON BROCADE	HELIOPSIS GOLDEN PLUME	AGAPANTHUS PATENS	LYTHRUM FIRECANDLE	HELENIUM GOLD FOX	PAPAVER GOLIATH	POLEMONIUM FOLIOSISSIMUM	HEMEROCALLIS PINK DAMASK
COREOPSIS VERTICILLATA GRANDIFLORA	SEDUM AUTUMN JOY	RUDBECKIA DEAMII	PHLOX MOTHER OF PEARL	IRIS LIGHT YELLOW OR BLUE	VERONICA BLUE FOUNTAIN	SOLIDAGO GOLDEN SHOWER OR LERAFT	HOSTA FORTUNEI PICTA
GERANIUM RUSSELL PRICHARD	POTENTILLA FIREDANCE	HEUCHERA SCINTILLATION	ASTER DWARF BLUE	SEDUM RHODIOLA	ACHILLEA MOONSHINE	ERIGERON PROSPERITY	SCABIOSA GRAMINIFOLIA PINKUSHION

BORDER PLAN FOR AN OPEN AND MAINLY SUNNY SITUATION

ONE SIDED 24' × 12' (32 SQ YDS) PLANTED 5 PER GROUP

This is for a one-sided border of the conventional style with a backing of some kind—wall, hedge or shrubbery. The tallest kinds are at the rear, and if you wish to follow such a plan, remember to leave ample space between the plants and the backing, as illustrated in the sketch on p.11. The **effective** width of the border is 12 feet, allowing for rear groups of up to 6 feet high when flowering. If you have only 9 feet width available, omit the back row of groups, and the next to it could also be omitted if your border can be no more than 6 feet wide. The four groups at each end are designed to grade down somewhat so that if a longer stretch of border is available, the plan can be elongated accordingly. This means that other kinds can be chosen to fill up the extra space, but you can use either of these four end groups to make the closure—reserving them for the ends.

It will be seen from the plan that the rear groups occupy rather more space than those near the front. Each group is designed to hold five plants of one kind to give a massing effect, but the taller and usually more robust kinds need more space than the shorter growing ones near the front. The irregular shapes of the groups need not be followed exactly. They merely indicate the need to avoid regimentation when planting, and the suggested position of each member plant of a group is indicated by a small x. These will also demonstrate the way in which greater space can be allowed between each group and the individual plants comprising a group. The border is planned to give a long display, with the first flowers appearing in April, and the last in October, but a different selection of plants could be made to provide more colour at any period between these months.

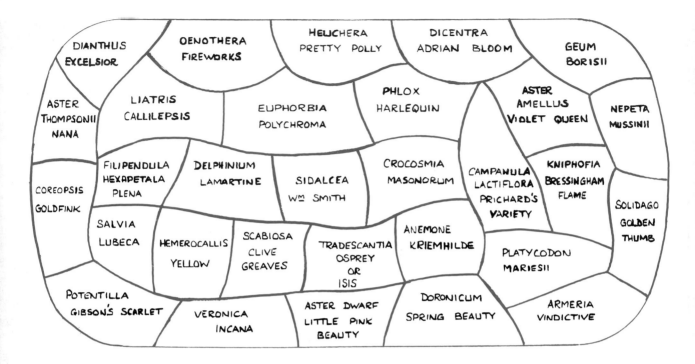

MIDGET ISLAND BED 18' × 9'

Although designed for a very small garden, this is typical of an Island Bed, regardless of size. It has all round access, and the tallest growing kinds are in the centre, where it will be noticed they occupy more spacious outlines than those around the perimeter. In this case some of the latter flower at only 9" or so high but the tallest in the centre run up to 4 feet. As with Border A., flowering is from April to October and colour contrasting or blending has been studied carefully. The use of graph paper in each case makes Border planning easy, because the inch squares in heavy outline represent a scale of 1" to 3 feet. There are approximately 18 square yards in the bed and thirty groups in three of a kind. For anyone wishing to vary the size or shape of such a bed to suit their own needs work on a average of five plants per square yard, but vary the area of groups according to height and spread. In this Midget, the outer groups are in some cases only 18" wide so that the plants form a compact but irregular edging.

The ends of the bed are rounded, but actual shape can be varied to taste. For a much larger bed, this same plan can be used, if colour massing appeals merely by increasing the size of each group from its present average of three fifths of a square yard. The total area would thereby be doubled if say six plants of a kind were used.

14

Island Beds at Bressingham against a background of mature trees; the foreground bed is shady, being on the north side of a shelter belt.

These are a few pointers and hints to emphasise the advice given in the text and it is quite easy to design one's own border. A larger bed could of course accommodate either a wider selection or larger groups, or both. It is purely a matter of choice, but there is no room for doubt that for effect, for ease of maintenance, the Island Bed form is far more satisfactory than the conventional one-sided border.

Plant names and origins

Whether one picks up a book or catalogue containing any wide variety of plants, they are listed under their Botanic or Latin names. This may be dispiriting or tedious for some, but not for those who, from love or experience of plants realise and accept that only by the use of such names —internationally known and accepted, could they possibly make sense. The question as to why such names have to be used is often asked by some who find them difficult, and as a preface I will attempt a brief answer.

Plants, no matter what they are, have to carry a first and second name at least, to simplify, identification and reference. The first name indicates the genus, and the second the species. Take **Campanula** as an easy example. This comes from the Latin for 'Bell', and indeed the common name is Bellflower. But there are in nature hundreds of species of Bellflowers or Campanulas, as well as varieties or cultivars which have been raised by human agency as hybrids or crosses between the species. It would be much more confusing to use English or colloqual to describe them, for **Campanula lactiflora** would then become the 'milky-flowered Bellflower'—plus the name of the variety. **C. glomerata nana lilacina,** would need the 'lilac flowered dwarf clustered Bellflower' to describe it—and these are only simple examples. Others would be quite impossible to anglicise.

All names have an explanation or meaning, though the origin of some generic or surnames are lost in antiquity. Some are Greek, others Latin or Latinised versions of a Common name. There is no need to delve deeply into origins, but many specific names give a clue to description. Those ending in **'oides'** mean that it has resemblance to some other plant, such as **'primuloides'.** Others give the colour—**'aureum'** for gold, **'album'** for white, **'roseum'** pink, **'rubrum'** red and so on. **'Latifolia'** means it has a broad leaf, **'macrantha'** a large flower in Greek, though **'grandiflora'** is the same thing in Latin. Where a name ends in **ii** or **iana** it is a personal tribute to someperson just as a surname like Rudbeck or Stokes are Latinised as generic names in **Rudbeckia** and **Stokesia** as a means of giving a name to a plant which had no higher claims.

Very many specific names give the place of origin—whether a country like Japan—**japonica** and **canadensis,** or an ancient State-like **macedonica** or **tyrolensis,** whilst others simply state that it grows wild in mountains **montana, alpina** or in woods **sylvatica** or in a damp place **lacustris, palustris** or **uliginosa** .

Once you get the hang of names, they can surprisingly enough become a source of interest in themselves. You can pick and choose, as it were, without bothering about those that have baffling connotations and derivations unless you wish. It is all a matter of not being afraid of them, of realising their importance and that most of them have purposeful meanings. No one uses any other name than Chrysanthemum, Nasturtium or Rhododendron, and there are many other examples of Botanic names being accepted by everyone without a second thought. This shows how even difficult names develop in the mind and become accepted as commonplace in themselves simply through common usage. If then this book is based on the correct internationally known nomenclature, something like a catalogue, it is all for the best, and will enable readers to come to terms with catalogues too—as well as the plants they offer for your pleasure.

PLANTS FOR SPECIAL PURPOSES

PLANTS FOR GROUND COVER

Alchemilla mollis
Bergenia in variety
Chrysogonum virginianum
Epimedium in variety
Lamium in variety
Nepeta mussinii
Prunella in variety
Pulmonaria in variety
Stachys lanata
Symphytum rubrum
Vinca in variety
Avena candida
Festua glauca

PLANTS FOR MOISTURE AND WATERSIDE

Aruncus sylvester
Astrantia in variety
Astilbe in variety
Caltha in variety
Gentiana asclepiadea
Filipendula in variety
Iris sibirica in variety
Iris kaempferi
Lythrum in variety
Monarda in variety
Polygonum in variety
Rodgersia in variety
Senecio in variety
Trollius in variety

PLANTS FOR DRY SHADE

Acanthus spinosus
Alchemilla mollis
Anaphalis in variety
Brunnera macrophylla
Campanula muralis
Epimedium in variety
Euphorbia — some varieties
Geranium in variety
Hylomecon japonicum
Iris foetidissima
Lamium in variety
Liriope muscari
Omphalodes in variety
Pachysandra terminalis
Polygonatum in variety
Polygonum affine in variety
Pulmonaria in variety
Stachys lanata
Tiarella in variety
Vinca in variety

PLANTS FOR FLORAL ARRANGEMENT

Acanthus in variety
Achillea in variety
Agapanthus in variety
Alchemilla mollis
Anaphalis in variety
Alstroemeria Ligtu hybrids
Astrantia in variety
Catananche caerulea
Chrysanthemum maximum in variety
Crocosmia masonorum
Delphinium in variety
Doronicum in variety
Erigeron in variety
Echinops ritro
Eryngium in variety
Gaillardia in variety
Gypsophila in variety
Heuchera in variety
Hosta in variety
Kniphofia in variety
Liatris callilepis
Lysimachia clethroides
Macleaya in variety
Nerine bowdenii
Polygonatum multiflorum
Polygonum amplexicaule
Polygonum bistorta superbum
Rodgersia in variety
Stachys lanata
Thalictrum in variety
Veronica virginica alba

Avena candida
Cortaderia argentea
Lasiogrostis splendens
Miscanthus japonicus

EXPLANATION OF SYMBOLS

Sun and Shade :
○ = Full sun. ◐ = Partial shade.
● = Full shade. ○ ○ = means that plants should be given the sunniest possible place with good drainage and are capable of withstanding drought.

Where no shade symbols are stated, it means that plants are fairly adaptable but prefer, as do the majority of kinds, a mainly open situation and need only ordinary soil, i.e. have no special requirements. Where two symbols are given, they are in order of preference.

ACHILLEA ○

ACHILLEA *filipendulina* 'Gold Plate'

These have no special needs beyond ordinary well drained soil and an open sunny position. All are increased by division, best in early spring or early autumn. A. 'Coronation Gold' is a smaller headed yellow, growing to a bushy 3 feet. A. *filipendulina*, usually offered under the name 'Gold Plate' is the tallest, reaching 4½ feet, with strong stems, carrying wide plate-head flowers June to August and pungent deeply cut leaves. Flowers hold their colour over winter, if cut and dried before they begin to fade on the plant.

A. *millefolium* 'Cerise Queen', grows from mat forming, rather untidy plants which need curbing or replanting every 2 to 3 years. Stems are filigree leaved about 2½ feet, tall, carrying loose heads June-August, which may need supporting. A. 'Moonshine' is a hybrid of great merit, having silvery filigree foliage and glistening flower heads on 20 inches stems, beginning late May and often with some in autumn too. Its parents A. *clypeolata* is a deeper yellow, but less reliably hardy and the lighter A. *taygetea* is less silvery and more erect at 2 feet tall. Double white Achilleas are, *Perry White* and *The Pearl*, but both spread rather quickly and may need support when in flower. All Achilleas are good for cutting, and if cut back in good time, sometimes flower a second time.

ACHILLEA 'Moonshine'

ACHILLEA 'Cerise Queen'

ACANTHUS ○ ◑

A. *spinosus* is the best known of
these imposing subjects. They need
space in which to be appreciated and
are vigorous enough to steadily expand,
with deep green leaves which are
not prickly, the individual flowers
are protected with a sharp spine.
These come on 4-5 feet spikes and
an established clump will continue
in flower more or less from June till
autumn. The roots of all Acanthus
are fleshy and deeply penetrating. A
site should be carefully chosen as
roots left in the ground broken off,
will sprout again. Plants are long
lived, drought resistant and not fussy
as to soil, but A. *mollis* is less free
to flower and needs a warm situation.
A. *longifolius* has handsome foliage
and 3-4 feet stems of lilac-mauve
flowers. The smallest is the slow
growing A. *perringii*. This has greyish
leaves and occasional spikes 12 inches
high of a pinkish shade.

ACANTHUS *spinosus*

ADONIS ○ ◑

A. ’*Fukujukai*’, is a newly introduced Japanese variety, which vies
with winter aconite for being the earliest flower in the garden. The
9-12 inches stems carry quite large golden flowers from February
to April according to season, followed by ferny foliage, but becomes
dormant from July onwards. The next Adonis to flower is the
beautiful double-greenish yellow A. *amurensis plena*. This grows
only 6 inches high, flowering March and April. The finest is
A. *vernalis*, which is April late May. It has glistening yellow flowers,
set in filigreed, shapely bushes 12-18 inches high, making a perfect
picture, and retaining its foliage till early autumn. All Adonis
are long lived but slow growing. They like light but deep soil,
neither wet nor dry and though old plants can be divided in autumn,
great care is needed to separate crowns with ample fibrous root, and
crowns should not be placed more than 2 inches below surface.
Because of their long period of dormancy, the position of plant
should be marked whilst leaves are still visible to avoid damage
when hoeing or digging.

ADONIS *amurensis* ‘Fukujukai’

ALCHEMILLA ○ ◐ ●

A. *mollis* is a splendid ground cover or
space filler for any but the driest, starved
conditions. The rounded glaucous leaves
mound up to 12-15 inches and above,
then from June to August come loose
sprays of sulphur yellow, to give a hazy
effect. There is a lushness about this
very adaptable plant, and it can be relied
on to smother weeds without itself being
a nuisance. It can be increased by seed
or division and is reliably hardy. Smaller
and scarcely less attractive species exist
which deserve recognition. A. *alpina*
grows only 6 inches, making good ground
cover, with yellow flowers just above,
and A. *splendens* with A. *hybrida* are
more grey-green with similar flowers,
both growing about 9 inches high. The
sprays of A. *mollis* are very effective as
a foil in floral arrangements.

ALCHEMILLA *mollis*

ACONITUM *napellus bicolor*

ACONITUM

The Monkshoods, show obvious relationship to Delphiniums,
and include some very good garden plants. They are easy to
grow, in sun or partial shade, but respond to good treatment by
flowering more freely where not starved. A mulching when
dormant, of fertilised peat or compost is helpful, but it pays
to lift and replant every few years. All unwanted roots should
be dug in deeply or composted. A. *napellus* has several variations
of which A. *'Bicolor'* is one of the best, with slender branching
spikes 3-3½ feet, tall from June to August. A. *'Newry Blue'* is an
earlier deep blue, growing to 4 feet tall. The shapely A. *'Bressingham Spire'* is outstanding for its symetrical spikes to 3 feet,
furnished with pretty glossy leaves. The flowers are violet blue,
from July to September and A. *'Blue Sceptre'* is of similar habit,
but a little dwarfer and has blue and white bicolor flowers.
For autumn flowering A. *fischeri* is attractive, and both this and its
variety A. *arendsii* prefer some shade where not too dry. The
latter is superb, with amethyst blue flowers topping strong 3½ feet,
stems, August to October. A *'Ivorine'* is distinctive on three
counts, not only has it a profusion of ivory-white flowers on erect
3 feet spikes, but it flowers early, from May to July. It has a
compact clumpy rootstock which promotes a shapely well foliaged
bushy habit and in a position not too dry, can be left for several
years. A. *orientale* is also worth mentioning because it is of similar habit and colour, though a little taller, and flowers from June
to August.

ACONITUM *fischeri*

AGAPANTHUS ○ ◑

A. *patens* is one of the best named varieties of what have become popular garden plants. All grow from a strong clumpy root, dividable in spring, and make strap like basal leaves. Flowers are carried in a clustered head, topping smooth stems 2-3 feet tall. They respond to good soil and to moisture during the growing season. Modern varieties are hardy, and all flower from early July to September. A. *'Isis'* is a deeper blue than *patens*, and A. *'Profusion'* is a rich light blue, very free to flower. Apart from the named varieties, A. *'Headbourne Hybrids'* are a strain that includes various shades of blue, with some variations in height as well. Being raised from seed they are of course less expensive, but any of the above are a good investment, both for garden decorations and for cutting.

AGAPANTHUS *patens*

ANAPHALIS ○ ◑

These are useful plants with silvery foliage and white near everlasting flowers, carried on loose heads. They are very adaptable, with dwarfer kinds able to give ground cover even in poor soil and in fairly shady places. They divide easily in spring and resent only wet conditions. A. *margaritacea* grows to 18 inches when in flower, but both A. *nubigena* and A. *triplinervis* are dwarfer with matted surface growth and 12 inches flower sprays. A. *yedoensis* is distinctive for being taller and more erect. The flower heads, capable of being dried, come on 2-2 ½ feet, stems in late summer, but though having no basal foliage, stems and leaves are silvery throughout the summer and autumn. Unlike the others, this spreads steadily below ground, but not to become a nuisance.

ANAPHALIS *margaritacea*

ALSTROEMERIA *"Ligtu Hybrids"*

For those who succeed in establishing a group or colony of these, there is a rich reward year after year. A site should be selected where soil is light, preferably sandy and deep, since the fleshy roots settle down at 8-9 inches below surface. They should not be placed in a bed or border with other flowers if this can be avoided, but more on their own against a wall facing other than north, or where sheltered from strong north winds. Old plants resent being moved, but young pot grown plants—or by direct sowing, will succeed best. Sow seed 1 inch deep in early spring or insert young plants, also in spring in well prepared soil, so that only green shoots are showing. It takes at least a year to become established sufficiently to flower, but once settled they are permanent and need only to be kept free of weeds. These can be sprayed safely in autumn, since roots are dormant from September to March.

ALSTROEMERIA 'Ligtu Hybrids'

ARTEMISIA ○ ◑

A. *lactiflora* is the only Artemisia grown solely for its flowers, which come as a plume on erect stems 4 feet high in late summer. Unlike most others, leaves are green and given the good and not too dry soil it prefers, they furnish the whole plant effectively. Plants are best divided in spring. Other Artemisias like dry sunny positions and have effective silvery grey foliage, with flowers of little or no account. Indeed these are best removed from such as the bushy, quick growing A. '*Lumbrook Silver*' and the daintier lacy leaved A. *discolor* (splendens) and A. *nutans*. A. *absinthium* grows erectly to 3 feet, with good foliage, but is less silver than the rather rampant A. *palmeri* and A. '*Silver Queen*'. These have stems rather than basal leaves, making them useful for floral arrangements, but the plants themselves sometimes need curbing lest they over run other subjects. All Artemisias are best planted and divided when necessary in early spring.

ARTEMISIA *lactiflora*

Spring in the garden

Although the peak period for colour amongst hardy perennials is from June to September, there is an ample range of spring flowering plants to make a brave show. Especially if these can be concentrated on one area of the garden. Such an area might be found where some shade exist from deciduous trees or shrubs which do not leaf until May. Bergenias, Brunnera, Dicentra, Euphorbia, Helleborus, Hylomecon, Lamiums, Polygonatums, Primulas (other than bog types) Pulmonarias, Vincas, etc., are all spring flowering and with bulbous subjects can be a source of great interest and pleasure, which lasts until perennials in more open positions claim greater attention.

ANCHUSA ○

A. *'Loddon Royalist'*, though brilliant
and useful for early flowering, this and
similar Anchusas may need supporting.
They also tend to leave a bare patch
once flowering is over by late June
and should be cut back to promote
fresh basal leaves. They grow from
3-5 feet high, from brittle fleshy roots
and as they resent wet soil in winter,
should be in a well drained spot.
Other varieties include the deep blue
A. *'Morning Glory'*, and the sky blue
A. *'Opal'*, but both these are tall.
A. *'Little John'* is only 20 inches, but
though flowering for longer, is less
spectacular. Full marks go to A.
angustissima both for brightness and
continuity in flower. Sprays spread
out and up to 15 inches, set with brightest blue flowers from early June to September, but unfortunately plants
exhaust themselves after 2-3 seasons.
It sets occasional seeds, but basal
cuttings in early spring can be taken,
whereas the taller Anchusas can only
be increased from root cuttings.

ANCHUSA 'Loddon Royalist'

ARMERIA ○

A. *maritima 'Vindictive'* is a multi purpose plant for it can be used
as a frontal border group, as an evergreen edging and in the rock-
garden. Of close mounded growth, the little drumstick flowers
come on 6-8 inches stems in June and July. There is a good white
form too, A. *maritima alba* and two that flower somewhat later.
These are the 9 inches A. *'Ruby Glow'* and A. *'Bloodstone',* 10-12 inches,
the latter being the deepest colour. The first two are the more easily
grown and also divide easily in spring or early autumn, but the taller
Armerias are best in full sun and well drained soil. The most
brilliant, but the most difficult to increase, from basal cuttings is
A. *'Bees Ruby'*. This makes a mound of broader, glossy foliage and
in June-July sends up 18 inches stems of quite large globular heads
of deep glistening pink. One other worth mentioning is A. *corsica*
on which the 9 inches stems carry salmon rose heads. All these
Armerias are long lived, given freedom from excessive soil wetness.

ARMERIA *maritima* 'Vindictive'

ANEMONE

ANEMONE *jap. hupehensis splendens*

ANEMONE *pulsatilla* (Pulsatilla vulgaris)

ANEMONE *jap.* 'Kriemhilde'

A. *japonica*.   Under this name are some first rate subjects for flowering in late summer and autumn.   They are long lived and trouble free in well drained soil, flowering for weeks on end.   In winter they die back to both woody and fibrous roots, which penetrate deeply and from these, increase is made whether left alone, or lifted to use as root cuttings.   Old plants however do not divide well and young pot grown stock give best results.   A. 'Profusion' is one of the dwarfer varieties with small double flowers, but not quite so deeply coloured as A. 'Bressingham Glow'.   Both grow under 2 feet. A. 'September Charm', clear single pink and A. 'Lady Gilmour' almost double, are a little taller, whilst A. 'Kriemhilde' is one of the best taller pinks, reaching 2½-3 feet.   The two best whites, with large flowers are A. 'Louise Uhink' and A. 'White Giant', both attaining 3-4 feet, and both with telling effect.

A. *lesseri* is a charming hybrid with lacy foliage and erect 18 inches stems, carrying soft rose-red flowers in May-June and often again in autumn.   It makes very little spread and should be grown in sandy soil.   A. *pulsatilla* is now correctly *Pulsatilla vulgaris* the Pasque Flower.   It grows with greyish lacy foliage coming as the deep cup shaped flowers open in April.   These have a hoary appearance. and can be had in mauve, purple and red shades.   They grow from 9-15 inches high and are followed by pretty seed heads.   Best grown in dryish soil, situated in sun, and increased only from seed.

AQUILEGIA ○ ◑

AQUILEGIA 'Mc Kana Hybrids'

ARNEBIA

ARNEBIA *echioides*

A. *echioides*. The 'Prophets Flower' holds a legend, Mahomet once stumbled in a rocky place and would have bruised his hand, but for the flower of this plant which cushioned his hand as he fell. The maroon spots on the bright yellow flowers are the imprints of the Prophets fingers, but though these fade in a few days, it makes little difference to the value of this unusual hardy plant. It grows only 9 inches high, from a tuft of tongue shaped leaves, the sprays opening in April and lasting for a few weeks. Plants are fleshy rooted, prefer light open soil and can be divided when old in early autumn—when occasionally a few late flowers are seen.

A. *'McKana Hybrids'* have the largest flowers and the best colour range of these garden favourites, growing to about 3 feet high, with long spurs. Although easy and adaptable, all Aquilegias tend to be short lived, but are easily raised from seed. Plants should however be a year old to flower freely and should be grown on, to plant in autumn, for the next season. Apart from such mixed strain as McKana, there are a few species in cultivation, in blue, white, purple, red and yellow, varying in height from 4 inches to 3 feet, but these are usually obtainable only from specialists, and from seed do not always come fully true to name and colour. Although the red variety A. *'Crimson Star'* is fairly reliable in this respect, along with the pink shades of A. *'Beidermeier'*, both growing about 18 inches high.

ARUNCUS ◑

ASCLEPIAS ○

ARUNCUS *sylvester*

ASCLEPIAS *tuberosa*

A. *sylvester*, is a majestic sight when in June the long creamy-white plumes are at their best. In good moist soil they may top 6 feet with abundant greenery and though the flowering period is rather brief, it lasts longer where shady as well as damp and the foliage remains attractive for the remainder of summer. Roots become large and are tough and woody, difficult to lift and divide, and a full grown plant needs at least a square yard of space, where it can be left alone for several years with an occasional mulch. There is a dwarfer, choicer Aruncus named *Kneiffii*. This has much slower, neater growth, with charming deeply cut foliage and slender plumes 2-2½ feet tall. It should be grown in a moist, shady position and responds to a humus rich soil.

A. *tuberosa*. If this plant, with its startling colour, were more adaptable it could be seen in every garden. But it is unfortunately rather faddy, disliking clay and chalky soils and needing light, sandy soil with perfect drainage and a sunny position. Its tap roots have a small terminal crown from which shoots appear in May, and their crowns are easily damaged when dormant. Stems reach 15-20 inches, branching at the top into a glistening orange head from July to September. A much easier species exists in A. *incarnata*. This makes stout and leafy bushes up to 4 feet high with waxy heads of deep rose pink. It will grow in ordinary soil, and can be divided in spring.

ASTRANTIA ○ ◑   ASTER

ASTRANTIA *maxima*

ASTER *thompsonii nana*

A. *maxima*. The most colourful of this curiously interesting genus, prefers a soil which does not dry out and makes a fairly rapid spread. The slender stems to 3 feet, carry a loose head of flowers from June to August. A. *carniolica major* has a tinge of both green and red in the otherwise whitish flowers, seen in the mass on 2½ feet, stems. A. *carniolica rosea* holds a deeper pink shade, but A. *rubra* is dark red, on stems only 18 inches high. The latter is slower to grow and needs good moist soils, but A. *involucrata* is very vigorous and free flowering, carrying a mass of somewhat shaggy whitish heads on 2½-3 feet, stems, from June to September. Astrantias have a charm of their own and given reasonable soil are effective despite their lack of brilliance. All can be easily divided in spring or early autumn.

To some the name may denote only the annual 'China Aster', but this genus includes an immense range of plants in which differences of height, habit and size of flower are very marked. Many of the species are worthless from a garden point of view, but as with so many, popularity of some has led to a great deal of breeding so that now, an original species bears little comparison with modern hybrids. This is particularly marked in the case of Michaelmas Daisies, but just because these have become so popular since breeding began 60 years ago, there is no excuse for neglecting species which have definite claims to garden worthiness. One of the objects of this book is to bring some of the less known plants to the notice of keen gardeners at a time when their attention is mostly drawn to popular hybrids. No one can blame nurserymen who go in for colour plate catalogues which tend to feature new varieties, because apart from catering for popular appeal, he is of necessity, out to make a living. He can only be blamed if purely for gain he offers a new variety to the public which is no better or different to some already in cultivation.

ASTER

ASTER *amellus* 'Violet Queen'

There are many other Asters with claims to garden worthiness apart from the more unusual Michaelmas Daisies, few of which are trouble free.

A. *thompsonii nana* deserves full marks on the points that really matter—of being long lived without making too much or too little growth, a long season in flower, and both colourful and graceful. It has a very compact root and the soft greyish shoots grow to form a bush about 15-18 inches high by the time flowering begins in July. From then till October, the yellow centred light blue daisies 1 inch across never cease. All it needs is well drained soil and a sunny position. Other species worth growing include A. *acris*. This too makes a compact, disease-free root and in August and September is smothered in small starry mauve flowers on wiry stems 2½ feet, high. There is a dwarfer form in A. *acris nanus* which is 18 inches-to 2 feet. A. *ericoides* is so named because of its resemblance to heather, though growing much taller. All varieties of this grow about 2½ feet tall, as strongly erect bushes and then in September-October are covered with tiny daisies. A. ericoides 'Brimstone' is sulphur yellow.

A. 'Cinderella' is light blue. A. *laevis* has starry lilac flowers in June and July on 2½ feet bushes but A. *linosyris*, is decidedly yellow, wiry stems to 2½ feet are topped by a head of tufty flowers and in this type the variety A. 'Gold Dust' is to be recommended. All the above are compact growing as plants, but easy to divide. A. *tongolensis* 'Berggarten' and A. *yunnanensis* 'Napsbury' are mat forming

ASTER

ASTER *amellus* 'Lady Hindlip'   ASTER *amellus* 'King George'.

and earlier to flower. They both have large blue, orange centred daisies on 15-18 inches stems in June-July, the latter being a week or two later than the former. A. *spectabilis* is another dwarf mat forming species, with leathery leaves on which come 12 inches sprays of really bright blue flowers in autumn.

A. *amellus*. This is an important but rather neglected group. No doubt this is due to them being slower growing, but this is in their favour and they do not suffer from the troubles of wilt and mildew which affect the more unusual Michaelmas Daisies. A. amellus flower from August to October, growing quite erectly with soft grey green foliage from a somewhat woody rootstock, and carry white heads of single flowers. They vary in height from

1½-3 feet, and unless pot grown, are much safer to plant in spring, which is the correct time for division. They are not fussy as to soil, so long as it is well drained and in an open position. The best known variety is A. 'King George', a lavender violet colour, but A. 'Violet Queen' is superior, a rich glowing violet colour and very free flowering. Pink shades in A. amellus tend to be less strong growing, but A. 'Lady Hindlip' and A. 'Sonia' are both of proven worth, the latter being the lighter colour. A. 'Otto Petschek' is a dwarf and free rich blue, and A. 'Nocturne' has a distinctive rosy-lavender shading. A hybrid between A. amellus and A. thompsonii has stood the test of time as a very fine plant. It is A. *frikartii* with open branching habit and large lavender blue flowers at 3 feet, high from July to October.

ASTER

ASTER *acris*

ASTER Dwarf *N. B.* 'Little Pink Beauty'

A. *Novae Belgii*, the true Michaelmas Daisy is now placed in two sections. The dwarfs are valuable for frontal groups and edgings and generally give excellent ground cover. Most of them have a vigourous spread and though to some extent susceptible to mildew, do not suffer like some of the taller N. B. section. There is now a wide range of dwarfs, varying in height from 9-18 inches, and one of the best is A. *'Little Pink Beauty'*, with semi double flowers, A. *'Alice Haslam'* is rosy cerise A. *'Blue Bouquet'*, A. *'Audrey'*, A. *'Lady in Blue'*, all strong blues, and rose red is seen in A. *'Dandy'* and A. *'Little Red Boy'*. A. *'Jenny'* is an outstanding violet purple, A. *'Rose Bonnet'* a rusty pink and A. *'Snowsprite'* is still the best white.

In recent years there has been a swing away from very tall Michaelmas Daisies and this is all to the good, for the taller they are, the more troublesome, through stem weakness. Over the past 20 years, probably well over 200 new varieties have been introduced and whilst some indoubtedly have added to range of colour and quality of flower, such a welter of varieties makes it difficult to provide a list of recommendations. With the emphasis still on the dwarfer, more shapely growing varieties, A. ,*Carnival'*, at 2 feet, semi double cherry red is worth growing, as is A. *'Melbourne Early Red'*. A. *'Royal Ruby'* is outstanding making a blaze of colour at barely 2 feet, and A. *'Royal Velvet'* a violet blue is also neat growing. A. *'Guy Ballard'* is a semi double deep pink, A. *'Sonata'* large flowered sky blue, and a good lavender blue exists in A. *'Percy Thrower'*, A. *'Crimson Brocade'* and A. *'Freda Ballard'* are semi double reds of proven merit and A. *'Tapestry'* is a mildew proof semi double pink. A. *'Lassie'* is an excellent pink also at 3 feet, and A. *'Marie Ballard'* is a large double flowered light blue. Though small flowered, the red A. *'Winston Churchill'* is still deservedly popular.

ASTER

ASTER *Novi-Belgii* 'Crimson Brocade'   ASTER *Novi-Belgii* 'Percy Thrower'

A. *Novae Angliae* is a less important section, having a limited colour range. Plants are sturdy but do not invade, and the stems are woody, long leaved. In dry or starved conditions these may shrivel before the head of finely rayed flowers open in autumn. A. *'Harrington's Pink'* is however, a charming colour and it is the only one that will drink when cut. A. *'September Ruby'* is worth a place for the colour is deep and glowing. Both grow to about 4 feet, but the wide lavender lilac flowers are carried on stems only 3 feet tall.

The attacks of mildew which sometimes affect the taller Michaelmas Daisies can only be prevented by spraying with a suitable solution before flowering. It becomes prevalent in dry weather, especially if there is a lack of sunshine and at the first signs of it, in June-July, a preventive spray used every 10-14 days, should keep plants free. Mildew only affects the current seasons growth and does not inhibit the plant itself, as does wilt. This is difficult to control and badly affected plants should be lifted and burned. A new stock from green tip cuttings, taken in spring is often recommended, but though no reliable rule exists, the safest course is to select wherever possible, stocks which a nurseryman is confident are virus free or varieties which are immune as some are.

ASTER *Novi-Angliae* 'Harrington's Pink'

33

ASTILBE

ASTILBE 'Fire'

These are so colourful, so perfect in form, with pretty foliage fully complimentary to the flowers, that it would be worth a little trouble to contrive the right growing conditions in a garden where they do not naturally exist. The plants themselves in all cases are tough and hardy, but without moisture and preferably some shade as well, they fall well short of the display of which they are capable. Moisture is more important than shade, yet this does not mean they should be treated as bog plants, but merely that they should not be allowed to dry out. Rich soil—plenty of peat and compost, with an annual mulch when dormant, will go a long way to making good any moisture deficiency and some shade or shelter from strong winds holds them longer in flower.

To enrich the soil is no problem, and a fairly simple method of providing extra moisture is easy to arrange as well. Tins—about quart size with a few holes punched in the side and bottom, can be inserted unobtrusively here and there between plants, to within an inch or less of the surface. One tin or a 12 inches long drainpipe will irrigate at least three plants and all one has to do is to fill this up with water during droughty weather every other day, and moisture will percolate to the thirsty roots more effectively than overhead watering. The same method can of course be applied for the other moisture loving plants mentioned in this book. Astilbes vary in height from 4 inches to 6 ft., and even the tallest need no staking. They go completely dormant in winter and from April onwards the leaves

ASTILBE 'Bressingham Beauty'

ASTILBE 'Cologne'

34

ASTILBE

ASTILBE 'Ostrich Plume'

appear and develop, all deeply cut and often purplish or bronzy green. Flowering begins in June and for several weeks they are very colourful indeed. In the middle height range of 2-3 feet, A. 'Fire' is aptly named, with even deeper reds in A. 'Glow' and A. 'Red Sentinel'. A. 'Cologne' is bright pink 2 feet tall, whilst A. 'Bressingham Beauty' is a little softer shade, growing to 3 feet. A. 'Amethyst' lilac purple, and A. 'Ostrich Plume' has pendant spikes of bright pink. These and several more including the 2-2½ feet whites A. 'Deutschland' and the dark leaved white A. 'Irrlicht' are extensively used for forcing as pot plants. But in the garden where height variations are important there should be room for such beauties as A. tacquetii superba. This grows to a stately 5 feet, with dark outspanning foliage and noble spikes of bright rosy purple with a long season in flower. Also tall, and excellent as waterside subjects, there is the rosy lavender A. davidii and the pale pink A. 'Venus' with A. 'Salland' a deeper pink.

Amongst these hybrid Astilbes are some that grow 1½-2½ feet, which carry dense plumes above mounded foliage. A. 'Fanal' and A. 'Etna' are red, rather similar to each other, and A. 'Federsee' is intense salmon pink. A. 'Mainz' is lilac rose and 'Intermezzo' a fine salmon pink.

The species A. simplicifolia has added its quota to the range of hybrids. The type is pretty, with graceful pink spikes 15 inches tall, but the variety atrorosea is superb, carrying sheaves of tiny bright pink flowers for a long time. There is white in this range and a charming dark leaved pink variety only 9 inches high, called A. 'Bronze Elegance'. For this and the salmon A. 'Dunkelachs', shade as well as moist humus is needed, but A. 'Sprite' is more adaptable. This is darkly leaved and the sprays carrying myriads of tiny flowers of pale shell pink make a most effective combination, growing 12 inches high and at least 12 inches across.

One other species should be mentioned—A. sinensis pumila. This has a creeping habit of fresh, crispy leaves, close to the ground and stumpy 12 inches spikes of a lilac rose colour, and it is less fussy about moisture than most. This along with A. tacquetii superba for a tall one, and A. 'Federsee' for medium height can be recommended as a trial selection for those who are dubious and not having grown them before. In my experience their moisture requirements are not so critical, but it should be added that only in summer droughts does this need for moisture exist, and even if witheld, the plant will survive for another season. Given an annual mulch, plants can be left down for years, but can also be divided when old and dormant without much difficulty.

ASTILBE tacquetii superba

BRUNNERA

BRUNNERA *macrophylla* (Anchusa myosotidiflora)

BRUNNERA *macrophylla variegata*

B. *macrophylla*. This was formerly *Anchusa myosotidiflora*, and the flowers have indeed a close resemblance to 'Forget-me-nots'. The sprays are however longer and more widely branched, developing up to 18 inches or so, by which time the 6 inches wide rounded leaves are forming a sturdy, mounded plant and when flowering has ended in June, fresh leaves continue all summer. It is an easy and adaptable plant for both sun and shade, not fussy over soil and readily divided. **B**. *macrophylla variegata* needs a little shade to give of its brightest best, for at least half the green of the leaves is replaced by a buff-almost primrose yellow shade. It grows almost as strongly as the type, and flowers just as pleasingly, but the variegation is perpetuated only by true divisions. This means that if dividing a detached root may sprout leaves and these will be green.

CATANANCHE

CATANANCHE *caerulea*

C. *caerulea*. This is another cut-and-come again plant and the papery cornflowers on single 2 feet stems have good cutting qualities. The fleshy rooted plants are amazingly free and long flowering, June to September, but such profusion takes its toll in exhaustion after 3 or 4 years. The 'Cupids Darts'—the folk name of this plant is best in sun and a well drained soil, and is very drought resistant. Increase is either from seed or root cuttings in spring 3 inches long, placed in a frame.

BERGENIA

BERGENIA 'Ballawley'

BERGENIA *cordifolia*

Where space needs filling almost regardless of soil and situation, Bergenias rank highly not only trouble freedom but for giving practically year round ground cover and a show of flowers. The latter in fact, appear as old leaves begin to fade in March, and by late May, when flowering comes to an end, there is a fresh cover of large glossy foliage. Plants expand from slowly advancing woody rhizomes or crowns at ground level, rooting downwards as they go. Their roots are fibrous and it is a very easy matter to curb any excessive growth. Single crowns planted in a row as an edging would become a yard wide in about 3-4 years to give complete cover, but naturally growth spread rate depends on soil conditions. Bergenias will grow under trees where fairly dry, in the open, or where fairly moist.

The flowers are at first rather like hyacinths, in a close packed, stumpy spike, but they open out in most kinds to become more branched. In the case of B. 'Ballawley', which is probably the finest of them all, stems can reach almost 2 feet. The B. *cordifolia* type is most commonly seen and neither this nor its slightly purple leaved form B. *cordifolia purpurea* exceed 15 inches high, with leaves less large than B. 'Ballawley'.

In recent years a number of named varieties have appeared, widening the range of colour. This includes silvery white in B. *'Silberlicht'*, near crimson is the dwarf growing B. *'Evening Glow'* (Abendglut) and a fine new pink is B. *'Margery Fish'*. Others are the salmon red B. *'Morgenglut'*, B. *Pugleys Pink'* and lilac in B. *'Pugleys Purple'*. B. *Schmidtii* is light pink with dense foliage.

Bergenias can be planted at almost any time and crowns with their woody rhizomes should be only just below surface. When dividing old plants it is best to discard any unthrifty or ugly roots.

CAMPANULA ○ ◑

CAMPANULA *carpatica* white

CAMPANULA *carpatica* blue

CAMPANULA *persicifolia*

Although blue is the basic colour in Campanulas or 'Bellflower' there is such wide variations in height and habit that they form an important asset in decorative gardening.   Most of them are reliable and trouble free and have no soil fads or fancies, adaptable to sun or partial shade.   They can be increased by division in spring but seldom come true when raised from seed.

Amongst dwarf growing kinds, C. *carpatica*, in shades of blue as well as white, grow neatly from 6 to 12 inches, making a show of upfacing bells from June to August.   C. *muralis* (portenschlagiana) is lavender blue, only 4-5 inches high, but has an amazing capacity for flowering and creeps slowly below ground. C. 'Stella', is really excellent, with starry flowers spreading out from a mounded plant often flowering twice—and can also be effective as an indoor pot plant. C. *alliariifolia* 'Ivory Bells' is of course white, a long lived variety of a free flowering species.   From June to August 18 inches sprays carry dangling bells, though they are not so large as the smoky blue flowers of C. *burghaltii* 18 inches, which also has a long flowering period. C. *glomerata* has several forms, but the flowers are clustered.   C. 'Joan Elliott' is violet blue, 18 inches for May and June. C. *glomerata nana alba* white, 18 inches, June to August and 'Purple Pixie' July to September.   The tallest is C. *glomerata superba*, which carries terminal violet cluster on 2½-3 feet stems in June and July.

C. *lactiflora* makes a more fleshy root and bears open heads of lavender mauve bell flowers in high summer on erect 3-4 feet stems.   There is also a white and the slightly pink C. 'Loddon Anna' which grows 4-5 feet.   C. *latifolia* grows strongly to 4 feet for June and July, the variety C. 'Brantwood' being violet purple and apart from a white variety there is the exquisite pale lilac blue C. 'Gloaming'. C. *persicifolia* is not so long lived as most, but during June and July makes a good show.   C. 'Telham Beauty' is the best blue, but a more reliable variety with the same form of saucer covered 3 feet spikes exists in C. 'Percy Piper', with rich blue flowers.   Finally, for those who like double flowers, the 2 feet C. 'Bernice', powder blue, is worth growing for the June-August period.

CAMPANULA *muralis* (*portenschlagiana*)

CAMPANULA ○ ◑

CAMPANULA
glomerata superba

CAMPANULA *latifolia* 'Gloaming'

CAMPANULA *lactiflora* 'Prichards Variety'

CENTAUREA ○

CENTAUREA *dealbata steenbergii*

CENTAUREA *macrocephala*

CENTAUREA *montana*

These are best described as perennial 'Cornflowers', though the wild 'Knapweed' is in fact a Centaurea too. They are easy to grow in any soil as well as being long lived, and respond easily to division. C. *steenbergii* has been popular for several years as the best form of C. *dealbata*. It has deep pink flowers in June and July, on very robust growth with greyish foliage, but the newer variety C. '*John Coutts*' has even larger flowers of a more delicate shade of pink. C. *macrocephala*, is a giant with large green leaves and stout 6 feet stems, carrying fluffy yellow flower heads from June to August. The species C. *ruthenica* is also tall but of more graceful appearance with dark green, deeply cut leaves and carrying lemon yellow flowers for a long season.

CENTAUREA ○

CENTAUREA *dealbata* 'John Coutts'

CENTRANTHUS

CENTRANTHUS *ruber coccineus*

C. *pulchra major* is handsome for its fine silver grey foliage and erect 3 feet spikes of large tufty pink flowers in June-July. Dwarf Centaureas have their place and nothing looks prettier than the 15 inches. C. *hypoleuca*, with its silver foliage and pink flowers and a much longer season than the May-June flowering C. *montana* varieties in pink, violet and purple. Other dwarfs, with good silver grey foliage are the 18 inches. C. *rigidifolia* and the 9 inches. C. *simplicicaule*. The latter does not flower very freely, but makes quite attractive ground cover. Both these have pink flowers in June-July and are tidier growing than the rather vigorous C. *montana* which is rather floppy and making a good deal of spread for all its short flowering season. Generally, Centaureas are sun loving plants and as is often the case with subjects having grey or silver foliage, prefer to be in dry rather than damp, ill drained soil. Another generalisation applies to Centaureas, which is that those that flower early are best divided or planted in autumn, whereas later flowering kinds are best in spring, but nursery grown plants can be moved at either season.

C. *ruber*. This is one of the easiest and longest flowering of 'old fashioned' hardy plants, one which will colonise from self sown seed. It will grow in any soil, however poor and even on a dry wall. When naturalized it is mostly the pinkish shade of colour, but the red, C. *ruber coccinea* is much brighter and more attractive. Plants flower at about 2½ feet from June onwards, but to prevent nuisance seeding, they should be cut back before seed ripens and falls to the ground. This plant as might be expected goes under more than one common name. It was botanically known as Valeriana and commonly called Valerian; certain medicinal properties are attached to Valerian, but this applies to those that still come under Valeriana. One of these has some garden value. It is V. *sambucifolia*—the Elder leaved Valerian, which grows to 5 feet or so, bearing heads of shell pink flowers from June to August. The heads are up to 9 inches across and much liked by bees and butterflies. The only fault with this plant is that in the moist soil it prefers, stems sometimes become top heavy and that one sometimes finds self sown seedlings coming up in or close to other plants. Otherwise it is an easy pleasing subject and quite adaptable as to soil, in full sun or partial shade. Another name for Centranthus ruber is 'Keys of Heaven' and it would be of interest to know the origin of such a name.

Summer Glory. These were the first six Island Beds to be made at Bressingham, and proved such a success that the author took in four acres of meadow, almost all on these lines. Some were moist or shady, others, like these, in the open and sunny. The majority of perennials prefer open situations. In the foreground to the right is the long flowering, long living *Acanthus spinosus*, and to the left *Geranium macrorrhizum* which has leaves smelling of Sweet Briar when crushed. In the centre are Phlox and to the right *Helenium 'Moerheim Beauty'.* The tall green behind makes a focal point, but later when in flower it is quite spectacular. It is the new *Miscanthus 'Silver Fern'*, growing six feet.

CHRYSANTHEMUM

C. maximum These may not appeal to everyone as border plants though they are mostly reliable enough and are widely used for cutting. Division should take place in spring. Modern varieties include doubles, such as the well known C. *'Esther Read'*, which grows 2 feet, but this is less reliable than the taller C. *'Wirral Supreme'*. Other doubles include C. *'Horace Read'* and C. *'Moonlight'*, but semi double or 'anemone centred' varieties are attractive, in which C. *'Aglaia'* and C. *'T. Killin'* are outstanding. Both these have flowers 4 inches across. The purely singles are the most common, and two good larged flowered varieties for those who like them are C. *'Everest'* and C. *'H. Siebert'*. Both grow to 3 feet. Hybridists have tried desperately to breed coloured Chrysanthemum maximum and I remember as a boy my father, who was a cut flower grower, saying that anyone who could raise a yellow 'marguerite' would make his fortune. I never tried, but others did, though such an Eldorado was never attained, despite varieties being introduced with such names as C. *'Cobham Gold'* and C. *'Moonlight.'* In these there is only a flush of pale yellow in the centre and the outer petals are still white. The arrival of C.*'Esther Read'* was however a landmark, for it was the first double to be raised. It has become so well known that this name alone is often used, and so popular for cutting that flowers are dyed to colour as required for sale.

CHRYSANTHEMUM *maximum* 'Wirral Supreme'

CAUTLEYA

CAUTLEYA *robusta*

C. robusta. This exotic looking subject grows strongly in a sheltered position and rich moist soil, not too alkaline. The roots are fleshy, with a central crown and radiating thongs, active only 2 inches deep and in cold districts a little covering from November to March is advised in case of severe frost. In early summer the reddish sheathed shoots develop to open out rather like compact growing 'Sweetcorn', but in July the yellow lipped flowers make quite a show against a back-cloth of lush greenery. Depending somewhat on moisture, height varies from 2½ to 4 feet and where happy there is an attractive display until well into autumn. Planting is best in spring and care must be taken not to injure the rather brittle roots and crowns.

CLEMATIS ○

C. integrifolia. The variety *hendersonii* is quite the best form of this unusual herbaceous, non-climbing Clematis. Though stems are somewhat lax, an established plant makes an attractive display from June to August and can be safely left to itself for many years. It is perfectly hardy and can be divided, as can the more robust C. *heraclifolia* types, of which C. '*Crepescule*' is a very good variety. The sky blue flowers on erect 3-4 feet bushes, have curled back petals, faintly perfumed and keep on for many weeks after mid-summer. These are two out of the ordinary subjects which please their owners and intrigue visitors unfamiliar with them.

CLEMATIS *integrifolia hendersonii*

CHRYSOGONUM

C. *virginianum*. This demure little plant begins flowering in May, and where happy, scarcely stops until October. To be happy, soil should be light, deep and not lacking in fertility, and with a low lime content. The plant grows neatly with soft green leaves above which the 9 inches flower sprays nestle, and apart from being fully hardy and long lived, divisions of older plants is easy. It is by division every 3 years or so, plus some soil enrichment when replanting that its longest flowering properties are encouraged.

CHRYSOGONUM *virginianum*

COREOPSIS

COREOPSIS *verticillata grandiflora*

COREOPSIS *grandiflora* 'Goldfink'

COREOPSIS *lanceolata*

The type most often seen is C. *grandiflora* usually raised from seed, but though flowering is profuse, plants seldom recover from one seasons exhaustive performance. Not so with other lesser known kinds. C. *verticillata* makes ample growth below ground with which to carry on for years and the growth above ground is quite delightful. The neat, narrow leaved bushes reach 1½-2 feet and from June to August are covered with a long succession of bright yellow flowers. The variety C. *verticillata grandiflora* is slightly larger and deeper coloured. C. *lanceolata* in the true form is most like the ordinary C. *grandiflora* but is also a true, long lived perennial. Growth is upright to 2 feet, and the 2 inch wide flowers come on slender single stalks. C. 'Goldfink' is a charming midget, with quite large flowers only 6-8 inches above close tufty plants. These have a small brownish centre zone. Flowering is profuse, from June to early September, but where any lack of basal growth is noticed by that time a cut-back to ground level should encourage it to begin, and with this renewed basal growth, no winter loss should occur. Spring division of the above Coreopsis is advised.

CROCOSMIA ○

CROCOSMIA *masonorum*

C. *masonorum*. For years this charming plant languished in obscurity because it was believed not to be hardy. Since 1963 however, its ability to withstand severe winter frost had been abundantly proved, and it has come in for the popularity it richly deserves. It grows from corms which build up so that one corm of a previous years making, remains attached to the new one above. Because the lower one acts as a storage reserve, they should not be separated, but left intact when planting to ensure flowering. Natural increase is made from rhizomes which form a shoot and subsequently, new corms, so that after two years in one position, there should be 3 or 4 which will flower as soon as they reach maturity. As with their relatives, Montbretia, Antholyza and Curtonus, Crocosmia prefers a sunny position and well drained soil. The sword-blade leaves stand erectly, reaching up to 2 feet by mid-summer by which time the slender stems 2½ to 3 feet tall are ready to flower, arching out at the top to make a telling display. Unlike some of its relatives, C. masonorum opens its flowers to the sun—and to the eye, remaining colourful for many weeks. Colour varies slightly from orange to flame, and apart from being so effective as a garden plant, it is outstanding for floral decorations. Quite recently, some crosses have been made between this and both Antholyza and Montbretia, which increase the colour range and widen the flowering period, and named selections will probably be introduced in 1972. Planting depth of these and C. *masonorum* should be 3 inches below surface, preferably in spring.

Even without such a background of trees, perennials provide infinite variety in form. The centre piece in this view of Bressingham Garden is *Heliopsis Golden Plume*, which flowers for three months.

DICTAMNUS ○

D. *fraxinella*. Another sun loving plant, with a deeply penetrating root which can withstand drought, and in any case needs well drained soil. Shoots emerge in spring, resembling Asparagus at first, but then develops into strong 2½-3 feet stems, with leaves resembling those of the Ash tree, from which the name fraxinella is derived. The flowers have prominent stamens and in hot weather a volatile oil is given off so that occasionally one can ignite it. This then, is the true 'Burning Bush', but the puff of flame is only momentary, and does not harm the spike. Flowering from June to August, Dictamnus will set seed and this is the only reliable means of increase, though resultant plants are slow to reach flowering size. Once established, plants resent being moved and division is therefore not to be recommended, for the roots are tough and the crowns tightly congested.

DICTAMNUS *fraxinella*

DELPHINIUM

DELPHINIUM Giant Pacific 'Blue Jay'

DELPHINIUM Giant Pacific 'Summer Skies'

Delphiniums do not come to perfection without effort. They need deep rich soil, are not immune to pests and diseases, and almost all need staking to avoid the havoc strong winds can cause. Specialists think nothing of producing spikes up to seven feet tall, but more recently it has been realised that for ordinary and modern gardens, such heights are troublesome to cope with, if not somewhat incongruous as well. This applies especially to named varieties which can only be propagated by division or basal cuttings. This makes them expensive to produce and to buy and since there has always been a demand for the more cheaply produced seed raised plants, a good deal of progress has been made towards achieving reliability as far as colours are concerned from seed. Some of these strains include the blood of shorter lived types and what are still known as D. 'Pacific Hybrids' contain some very rich colours, including pinks and purples, as well as true blues. They can be sown under glass and by keeping them on the move, they will flower later in the same year, but are not likely to live more than 2 or 3 years, as a general rule. The longer lived mixtures or strains from seed will mostly survive for five years and occasionally for much

DELPHINIUM Giant Pacific 'Hybrids'

longer, but for long life the vegetatively produced varieties are supreme provided the soil is well drained and plants are kept healthy and free from slug damage. Planting is safest in spring just as new growth begins and when dividing old plants, healthy shoots with young fibrous roots should be selected, discarding any woody or damaged growth.

D. 'Lamartine' is one of the Belladonna varieties. These have smaller flowers on more branching, slender spikes than the more usual and mostly taller varieties. They too flower in June and July, but need less space and are generally quite reliable and good for cutting. Apart from Lamartine, there is the sky blue D. 'Blue Bees' and the deep violet blue D. 'Wendy' and a clear mid-blue D. 'Peace'. D. 'Pink Sensation' could also be included here. It is a charming long flowering plant, but not very robust, growing only 2½-3 feet high from a fairly small plant.

This, and the Belladonnas mentioned above, must be increased by division or basal cuttings in spring.

No list of varieties in the taller Delphinium varieties need be made. They can only be obtained from specialists whose catalogues will give full descriptions for each, but full account should be taken of height. It is too late, often enough, to stake Dephiniums when flower buds are showing, because they are then already weakened by wind or by their weight. Nowadays there are named varieties, that do not attain more than a modest 4 feet or so, and these are easier to cope with.

The D. 'Pacific Hybrids', as seed or as seed raised plants of flowering size can be had as a mixture, or in shades of a given colour. D. 'Astolat' is in pinkish shades, D. 'Black Knight', representing the deepest violet blues, D. 'Blue Jay', mid-blue with white eye. D. 'Cameliard', lavender blue, D. 'King Arthur', purple and D. 'Galahad', white.

DIANTHUS o

DIANTHUS *caesius*

DIANTHUS *deltoides* 'Flashing Light'

DIANTHUS Dwarf single

'Pinks' never fail to please, not only because of their bright colours, but because most of them are scented. All kinds like sun and well drained soil and are often happy in thin chalky, stoney, or sandy conditions. With none of them exceeding 18 inches or so in height, they come in for frontal positions and some of the neater growing ones, make excellent edging subjects to a path, rosebed or south facing shrubby border—apart from a rock garden. From seed, a mixture can be expected, not so much in height as in colour, but this, whether home raised or by purchase, is often no disability, for all flower at much the same time, between early June and August. Those that grow no more than about 6 inches high are sometimes called Alpine Hybrids, but are none the less fully adaptable at the front of taller perennials. They can be had in both double and single strains or varieties, but generally the doubles are taller and come under the true category of Pinks. In these, the old fashioned D. 'Mrs. Sinkins', with double white flowers is still popular as is the pink flowered D. 'Excelsior', with D. 'Mrs. Pilkington', an excellent light pink and D. 'Ipswich Crimson' a good double red. D. 'Sam Barlow' is white with a crimson flecked centre, whilst D. 'Paddington' is pink, with a dark red centre fleck. These named varieties are increased by cuttings or by divisions in autumn. Straggly shoots should be tucked in and well firmed so as to encourage rooting along the stem. Taller single flowered varieties can be obtained in a good colour range as a mixture from seed, and these give a long season in flower with heights up to 18 inches. For a really dwarf one, with deep green foliage, the D. *deltoides* 'Flashing Light' is outstanding the foliage makes a carpet, but the small flowers on 4-6 inches stems are so profuse that the plant becomes a blazing red cushion of colour from June to August.

DICENTRA ○ ◑

DICENTRA *spectabilis*

'Bleeding Heart', 'Dutchmans Breeches' and 'Lady in the Bath', are names for D. *spectabilis*, which is one of the loveliest of all plants for late spring and early summer. The root is ugly with its fleshy fangs, but the shoots emerging from it enhance their early promise as they unfurl with fresh looking deeply incised leaves. Through these arch cut branching stems to 2 feet or so, from which dangle the locket like flowers to which such folksy names have been given, though to see how the last mentioned of these applies, the flower has to be held upside down. Flowering lasts for several weeks from May onwards and for all its fragile appearance, the plant itself is fully hardy. It's only needs are for reasonably good well drained soil, and to be sited where the strongest winds do not harry it. Old plants can be increased by very careful division, for both roots and shoots are brittle. D. *eximea* and its varieties make some spread, with less fangy roots and make a mound of pretty glaucous foliage. The type is a rather dull rose pink, but in the variety D. *'Adrian Bloom',* the individual flowers are much larger and of a ruby red shade, on sprays 15 inches high, from May to July and often longer. D. *'Bountiful'* is also large flowered, but less richly coloured, whilst D. *eximea alba*, is white and only 9 inches tall. These Dicentras divide easily, best in early autumn and benefit thereby if the ground is dug over and enriched every 3-4 years.

DICENTRA *eximea* 'Adrian Bloom'

DORONICUM ○ ◐

DORONICUM *caucasicum* 'Spring Beauty'

DORONICUM 'Harpur Crewe'

ERIGERON 'Foerster's Liebling'

These too, are spring flowering and combine well with Dicentras for colour effect. They are amongst the easiest of plants to grow and though already popular, no garden should be without them, since they make a splash of colour which, with the variety existing, cover the months of April, May and June. The first to flower are the dwarfest D. *'Gold Dwarf'*, having yellow rayed daisies on 6 inches stems from early April. This is quickly followed by the unique double variety D. *'Spring Beauty'*. Flowers show yellow in the bud, but open out into perfectly formed doubles of rich yellow as the branching stems develop, till it reaches 15-18 inches in May. This is one of the most outstanding introductions in recent years, but for those preferring single flowers, the 18 inches D. *'Miss Mason'* has them 3 inches across from mid-April till June. D. *'Harpur Crewe'* does not flower until May and sends up 3 feet stems, topped with finely rayed flowers 3-4 inches across. All Doronicums grow from mat forming plants that divide easily and are improved by replanting every 3-4 years. They can be planted at any time after flowering and although they respond to good soil, they are very adaptable and trouble free.

ERIGERON ○

ERIGERON 'Darkest of All'

These are valuable members of the Daisy Family, which always flower freely during the June-August period. Good drainage is their main requirement and a preference for being planted —or divided when necessary in early spring rather than autumn. Nowadays one scarcely ever sees species being used in gardens because so many more colourful hybrids have been introduced. Outstanding amongst these came from Karl Foerster, the famous German hybridist who was still active until his death in 1970 at the age of 97, E. 'Foerster's Liebling' is therefore appropriately named, and it must have gladdened him to distribute a really reliable pink Erigeron with flowers almost double, at a modest height of 18 inches. E. 'Rose Triumph', a little lighter in colour, is another of Foerster's darlings, and though E. 'Prosperity' was one of my raising, it has exactly the same habit of a sturdy clumpy plant, the 18 inches flower stems carry semi double mauve blue flowers in June and July. Other good Erigerons exist in the upstanding 2 foot E. 'Amity', with lilac rose single flowers, and the single pink E. 'Charity'.

E. 'Darkest of All' grows erectly, with violet blue rayed flowers, as has the dwarfer long flowering E. 'Dignity'. E. 'Lilofee', is a taller semi double mauve blue, E. 'Gaiety' is single deep pink and E. 'Sincerity' a single lavender blue. The dwarfest of modern hybrids is E. 'Dimity', which with others ending with 'ity' were names I chose. This has soft foliage and stems radiate to make a low mound only 10 inches high, carrying firstly orange shaded buds which turn to pink as they open. This variety needs to be cut back as soon as ever flowering is over and better just before, in order to promote the renewed basal growth it needs for overwintering.

One species worth mentioning is E. simplex, not only because it is white flowered, but because it flowers in May and June, and has a very neat habit, with a height of under 12 inches.

ECHINOPS ○

ECHINOPS *ritro*

EPIMEDIUM ◑ ○

EPIMEDIUM *rubrum*

The 'Globe Thistle' is an attractive plant, with its grey and jagged foliage, and stems carrying rounded blue flower heads from midsummer onwards. Some kinds are rather too coarse growing for small gardens, but the more compact are not only effective, but can be left alone for years with no attention beyond cutting back one seasons growth when faded, in readiness for the next to come. Any but damp soil will suffice and they are drought resistant, whilst flowers are of value for cutting.

The best known is E. *ritro* and at 3-3½ feet is imposingly erect, without being too tall as is inaptly named E. *humilis*, of which E. 'Taplow Blue' is a variety with paler blue flowers than ritro. E. 'Blue Cloud' is large flowered, 4-5 feet and E. 'Veitch's Blue', of good colour at a similar height. The little known E. *gmelini*, is 2½ feet free flowering and neat growing, the colour being slightly lighter than ritro. The larger Echinops make massive plants and need ample space, but all will divide with a spade or knife and will come from root cuttings, as well as from pieces of root accidently left in the ground.

In the upsurge of interest taken in ground covering plants, Epimedium have come to the fore in recent years. They have very pretty foliage and a slowly creeping habit below ground which affords a canopy of greenery—often tinged bronze, lasting until late autumn. The new leaves follow the flowers. These appear in early spring, on short sprays and although individually small, they are capable of making quite a show with their starry formation and bright colours. Although adaptable, Epimediums respond best to good soil where shady, but not excessively dry. Dryness can be offset by using a coating of peat or compost ½ inch to 1 inch deep, over the surface during winter, for they are not deep rooting plants and when lifted come up as a mat of fibrous rooted crowns which divide quite easily. This is best done in autumn. E. *rubrum*, is compact growing with flower stems 9 inches high and foliage about 6 inches. E. *macranthum*, is of similar height, but the brighter pink E. *Rose Queen*, is dwarfer still. E. *youngianum*, with pink flowers is not so showy as the white form E. *youngianum niveum*, which is a much sought after subject. All the foregoing are grouped as being the choicest and slowest to spread, but the following are stronger growing and more adaptable. E. *perralderianum* is the strongest growing of them all, having bronzy yellow flowers on 12 inches sprays and leaves 9-12 inches above ground. E. *pinnatum* is canary yellow of similar height, with the variety E. *elegans*, the best form. E. *cantabrigensis* is a hybrid, having dense foliage, following browny orange flowers on 10 inches sprays, and the bright orange sprays of F. *warleyense* are really showy.

EUPHORBIA ○

E. *polychroma* (epithymoides) is very adaptable, and begins to make a show in early spring with its clustered sulphur yellow heads. These reach 18 inches by the time they fade in May and plants become a green leaved bush until autumn. It is a sterling plant, long lived and trouble free, as is the much taller, later flowering E. *palustris*. This grows to 3-4 feet and prefers soil not too dry, but E. *griffithii* 'Fireglow', has a slowly creeping habit below ground. Given an open sunny position it grows erectly to 3 feet, by June the intense burnt orange heads begin to fade and merge into green. These three are suited to ordinary open positions, and can be increased by autumn or spring division. E. *amygdaloides*, E. *robbiae* and E. *macrostegia*, are somewhat similar in making fairly rapid ground cover foliage in sun or shade, about 9-12 inches high, and carrying loose heads of sulphury flowers. The smaller, silvery blue leaved E. *cyparissias*, with yellowish heads only 9 inches high. E. *wulfenii*, and the very similar E. *characias* are shrubby and can only be increased by seed. Seedlings occur and it takes 2-3 years to reach flowering size at 3 feet, covering itself in spring with spectacular lemon yellow heads. These will grow in dry soil. The silver-blue ground hugging E. *myrsinites*, needs a sunny spot, well drained, and the foliage has year round attraction, and makes a large head of sulphury-yellow flowers in spring.

EUPHORBIA *polychroma* (epithymoides)

EUPHORBIA *griffithii* 'Fireglow'

EUPHORBIA *myrsinites*

Perennials are not so much in evidence at the end of the Dell Garden at Bressingham. Alpine plants grow atop the flint wall flanking the pool, and the background of specimen Conifers all adds to variety which can be achieved in small gardens too.

GENTIANA ○ ◑

GENTIANA *asplepiadea*

Although associated in most peoples minds with Alpine gardening Gentians are a very large genus, and include some that grow 3-4 feet high to include yellow as well as blue. There are also a few, taller than the truly Alpine species, which should be included here. G. *asclepiadea* is the Willow Gentian, so named because its slender 2 feet stems have willowy leaves. The blue trumpets, somewhat clustered towards the top, are deep throated, and make an attractive display from July to September. Shades of blue vary a little and apart from the bright G. *'Knightshayes'* variety, there is a white. G. *septemfida* and other of its kin are dual purpose—for rock garden or border. They have deep roots and tufty green shoots above the ground which develop into leafy but rather lax stems from 6-10 inches high and carry clusters of brilliant blue trumpets from June to August. These summer flowering dwarf Gentians will grow in any good soil regardless of lime content, but G. *asclepiadea* not only prefers neutral or acid soil, but likes some shade as well, especially where not dry. Seed is the only safe method of increase. Old plants resent being moved and young pot grown stock are best to use.

ERYNGIUM ○

ERYNGIUM *tripartitum*

ERYNGIUM *bourgatii*

ERYNGIUM *variefolium*

The name 'Sea Holly' applies only to E. *maritimum* and though pretty, it is a plant that does not take to inland gardens. Other species will grow strongly from fangy roots in well drained soils to give a charming display of bluish flower bracts, often with stems blue as well. One of the prettiest is E. *bourgatii*, which has silvery, deeply cut and somewhat prickly foliage. It has erect shortly branched stems to about 2 feet carrying quite large silvery blue flowers above a spikey base. E. *amethystinum* is green leaved, but the flowers are deep blue, whilst E. *tripartitum* carries a sheaf of smaller blue flower on 3 feet stems. E. *planum* is strong growing but less blue, but E. *variefolium* has very pretty marbled foliage close to the ground and erect branching stems to 2½ feet of blue flowers, E. *giganteum* is silvery all over and though very effective, it dies after flowering and seedlings for replacement must be a matter of forethought. There are a few entirely green species, with fearsome looking evergreen foliage in large rosettes. E. *bromeliaefolium* and E. *serra* are two of them, which may appeal to some and like most species are not difficult and are long lived.

57

ECHINACEA ○

ECHINACEA *purpurea* 'Bressingham Hybrids'

E. *purpurea*. The purple 'Cone Flower' is an offshoot from the Rudbeckias and is sufficiently distinct to warrant generic rank. The degree of reflex in the petals varies, as does the colour, for apart from purple shades, of varying intensity, there is a white variety. By far the most spectacular are those with broad petals in which a warm rosy to salmon purple is present, as seen in E. *'Bressingham Hybrids'*. These vary but little in colour and form, being of the same breed as the named variety E. *'Robert Bloom'*. They are outstanding for vigour, erectness and freedom to flower, all growing about 3 feet high and flowering from July to September. An old variety E. *'The King'* is still offered, but the colour is comparatively dull on stems that do not always stand erectly. E. *'White Lustre'* is unusual, having drooping petals and a yellow cone at 3½ feet. To grow these plants well, a sunny position and deep light soil is preferred. They can be left alone for several years where happy, but if dividing, March-April are the best months.

FILIPENDULA ◑

FILIPENDULA *ulmaria aurea*

It would be misleading to apply the common name 'Meadowsweet' to all the Filipendulas, since it applies only to the wild F. *ulmaria*, of which only one form is of real garden value. This is the golden leaved F. *ulmaria aurea* which, given fairly moist soil with some shade, makes a most attractive mound from its foliage alone, from April to October. The flowers are non descript and the 2 feet stems are best cut back once they reach full height to promote renewed foliage. F. *palmata rubra* (syn. purpurea) needs similar conditions of shade and moisture, and the leafy bushes are topped with glowing rosy crimson heads 3 feet high in June-July. This is a choice plant, but F. *elegantissima*, with glistening pink is more robust and less in need of shade. It grows to 4 feet and there is a similar but much dwarfer pink species in F. *palmata elegans*. F. *digitata nana* makes hummocky growth, with deep green fingered leaves and has deep red flowers on 10 inches stems from June to August. All these are responsive to moisture and plenty of humus, but have a rather brief period in flower if this is denied. All are easy and safe to divide in autumn or spring. The one Filipendula suitable for ordinary soil, even if dry, is F. *hexapetala*, but the type is much inferior to F. *hexapetala plena*, which carries dazzling heads of white flowers in June-July. The 2 feet stems rise from deep green carrotty foliage and the roots are somewhat woody. F. *hexapetala grandiflora* grows 2½-3 feet and the heads of creamy white are slightly scented, as well as being attractive to bees. The two last named are long lived and trouble free, but mulching as for Astilbes, is advised for the remainder.

FILIPENDULA *palmata rubra (purpurea)*

FILIPENDULA *hexapetala grandiflora*

GAILLARDIA ○

GAILLARDIA 'Croftway Yellow'

GAILLARDIA 'Goblin'

GAILLARDIA 'Wirral Flame'

An inherent fault in Gallardias is that they tend to flower themselves to death. This is less likely to happen on poor soils than in rich strangely enough, and the best way to avoid this is to cut hard back in August, so as to promote renewed basal growth. Flowering begins in June and for several weeks there is a real spate of flowers, soft petalled in bright yellow-red combination. Stems are apt to be floppy or top heavy, although seldom taller than 2½ feet. The roots are capable of producing new shoots, and if and old plant is spaded off 2 inches below ground, ample young plants will appear in due course. Old plants do not divide well or move well, and from seed a mixture of colours can be expected. Named varieties, raised from root cuttings include the self coloured G. *'Croftway Yellow'*, G. *'Ipswich Beauty'*, deep yellow with brown red zone, G. *'Mandarin'* a glowing flame red, with only an outer margin of yellow, and G. *'Wirral Flame'* deep browny red. G. *'Goblin'* is a pygmy, only 10 inches high, but with almost full sized flowers of yellow zoned brown red.

GERANIUM ○ ◑

GERANIUM 'Russell Prichard'

Practically all true Geraniums are fully hardy; since the so called Geraniums for indoors or summer bedding are Pelargoniums. There are more garden worthy kinds of Geraniums than most gardens could find room for and as a genus it is both varied and very adaptable, both to soil and situation. In general, they are best increased by division and this can be done in either autumn or spring. Those that prefer sun are the dwarfest and G. 'Russell Prichard' makes a mounded carpet of soft grey green set with intense magenta pink cups from June to September. With a similar surface spread of growth G. wallichianum 'Buxtons Blue' has pretty lavender blue, pale centred flowers for much of the latter half of summer. G. candidum a charming white species is also fairly prostrate or cushioning but both G. grandiflorum and G. macrorrhizum have a leafy spread, extending its roots in keeping. The former has blue flowers, and the latter no great show of pinkish saucers but the foliage has a 'sweet briars' perfume when crushed. G. sanguineum has dense growth above ground from clumpy plants and magenta flowers and there is an excellent pink variety in G. sanguineum lancastriense splendens. These rise to about 12-15 inches and make a bright show from June onwards. The varieties of G. endressii are very vigorous, mounding up to 18 inches and have pink salvers. A hybrid named G. Johnsons Blue makes a fine splash in June-July, about 15 inches high and G. wlassovianum, with a lavender blue flower, carries on flowering on cushioned growth, till late August. G. renardii is notable for its greyish puckered leaves densely canopied 12 inches high all summer, following a brief show of prettily veined pale lilac cups. G. sylvaticum flowers in May and June, the best blue being G. 'Mayflower' with an attractive white G. album. G. ibericum (platypetalum) grows bushily to 2 feet, with deep blue heads of cup shaped flowers in June-July, and G. 'Claridge Druce' has a vigorous spread of lilac pink flowers and is useful for covering odd corners even if shady. G. phaeum—the 'Mourning Widow' has small but darkly purple, almost black flowers in early summer, will also grow in shade. G. pratense, the 'Meadow Cranesbill' has a good blue form in G. 'Mrs. Kendall Clarke', and these are double flowered forms, both blue and white. G. armenum (psilostemon) is fiercely brilliant and will grow to nearly 3 feet where moist, making a display from June to late August, with a slightly less violent colour in the otherwise similar G. 'Bressingham Flair'. This is a wide selection, though still not complete, it should be sufficient to stimulate greater interest in these valuable hardy perennials, many of which have been undeservedly neglected in the past.

GERANIUM ○ ◑

GERANIUM *armenum*

GERANIUM *sylvaticum* 'Mayflower'

GERANIUM 'Johnson's Blue'

GERANIUM *sanguineum*

GEUM ○

GEUM 'Lady Stratheden'

GEUM 'Rubin'

GEUM 'Mrs Bradshaw'

The best known Geums are the double red G. 'Mrs. Bradshaw', and the double yellow G. 'Lady Stratheden', but unfortunately these have only a short life. They can only be raised from seed, and though plants will flower well the following year after sowing, begin to deteriorate from then on. Both grow 20-24 inches giving a colourful display from late May to August. There are however other Geums which have a perennial constitution, forming clumpy growth which will divide easily. Division every 2 or 3 years discarding old woody growth, greatly improves flowering freedom and continuity. Geums are not fussy as to soil and can be planted in autumn or early spring . G. borisii is a first rate little subject, with densely mounded leaves and 12 inches sprays of intense deep orange flowers in May and June. G. 'Rubin', along with G. 'Red Wings' are semi double red, flowering at 2 feet from early June to well into August. Of similar habit, G. 'Fire Opal' is flame coloured and G. 'Dolly North' is orange yellow. G. 'Georgenberg' is demure, only 10 inches with deep yellow flowers somewhat pendant, begins in May, continuing for many weeks and reliably perennial. G. rossii, is very distinct, with pretty carrotty foliage from neat tufty growth, and butter yellow flowers on 9 inches sprays from May to July.

GYPSOPHILA ○

GYPSOPHILA *paniculata* 'Bristol Fairy'

GYPSOPHILA 'Pink Star'

The charming folk name of 'Baby's Breath' applies to the single flowered C. *paniculata*. From a sturdy top or fangy root this makes a considerable summer spread of somewhat tangled twiggy branches forming a cloud of tiny white flowers.

G. 'Bristol Fairy' has larger, double flowers and both will reach 3 feet high and as much in diameter when at their best.

G. *compacta plena* (Bodgeri) is like a smaller edition of the latter and covers the same period in flower from June to late August. This is also the period for two pink varieties, but it must be said that both the 18 inches. G. 'Pink Star' and the prostrate G. *Rosy Veil* the colour is but faint. They are however good perennials capable of covering a fair amount of space and having a long period in flower.

All Gypsophilas like sunny well drained conditions and as the generic name states, they revel in chalky soil. The single G. *paniculata* comes only from seed.

HELENIUM ○

These are amongst the indispensibles but so often one sees them in gardens looking starved and bedraggled. There are usually two reasons for this. Either they are old, over tall varieties, or have been left so long attented that the plants have become lacking freshness and vigour, producing more stems than the roots are able to support. The result is that the stem leaves shrivel by flowering time and the flowers themselves are small and soon fade.

The remedy is of course, to go in for shorter growing varieties if this is a fault, and otherwise to divide and replant after digging and enriching the soil. This is good practice with all Heleniums every 3-4 years and well worth the trouble. When dividing use only the outer younger shoots which easily break away from the rest—an operation best done in spring.

Heleniums provide some very rich colouring nowadays and amongst the newer varieties H. 'Gold Fox' is outstanding, with its streaky orange and flame-brown shading. It grows to about 3 feet, as do the very attractive and sturdily upright H. 'Coppelia'. In the same height range and in the same June-August period H. 'Moerheim Beauty' is a favourite, with bronzy red flowers and with H. 'Mahogany' a similar colour but later flowering and H. 'Golden Youth' a warm deep yellow, there is a good selection at this intermediate height. For August-September flowering H. 'Baudirektor Linne' can be recommended as a tawny orange-red. H. 'Bruno' is close to being mahogany red, and H. 'Butterpat' a rich yellow. These attain 4 feet which is plenty tall enough for any Helenium, for where hemmed in conditions prevail the taller they grow the more likely they are to need support since the flowers are carried on terminal heads, tending to make them top heavy if stems are weakened by lack of air and light.

HELENIUM O

HELENIUM *pumilum magnificum*

HELENIUM 'Coppelia'

The dwarfest Heleniums are the earliest to flower—and often the longest flowering.

H. *'Crimson Beauty'* is more brown than red, but the flowers open on bushy leafy plants barely 2 feet high. H. *'Wyndley'* has larger flowers in which orange yellow is streaked with reddish brown, also with a bushy habit little more than 2 feet. H. *'pumilum magnificum'* is 2½ feet and the flowers are self coloured butter yellow. All these three begin early in June and continue well into August, in any good garden soil.

HELENIUM 'Gold Fox'

HELIANTHUS ○

The name literally translated from the Greek, means 'Sun Flower', but the perennial kinds have little resemblance to the rather grotesque annual species. There are some perennial kinds which are very weedy, spreading quickly below ground, and sending up stems 5-6 feet high with single yellow flowers on top. These are simply not worth growing and are a menace amongst better subjects. It is far better to fork them out and insert in the compact rooted kinds, which include double flowered varieties and have a much neater, though still robust, bushy habit. The 5 feet H. 'Loddon Gold' is a fine double variety with flowers up to 4 inches across, covering the plant on short stems. H. 'Triomphe de Gand' is semi double, of similar height, and of a similar rich yellow colour. It is a finer plant than any of the purely single flowered varieties and to be correct, it should be described as Anemone centred rather than semi double. Helianthus are easy in any ordinary soil, but do respond to reasonably good treatment such as an occasional mulch. Division is best in spring, but some thinning out should take place rather than allow overcrowding to spoil them.

HELIANTHUS *multiflorus* 'Loddon Gold'

This shows the effect of planting acording to height. It is an Island Bed with the twenty inch *Erigeron Foersters Liebling* at the front, ranging up to the five foot *Thalictrum augustifolium* behind, and then down again the other side to.dwarf kinds.

HELIOPSIS ○

HELIOPSIS 'Incomparabilis'

HELIOPSIS 'Golden Plume'

These are fairly closely related to Helianthus, but though yellow is their only colour, there are variations in both theme and form. For trouble freedom they rank highly, as they do for their long flowering qualities. Their only basic need is for a reasonably good soil, regardless of being heavy, light, acid or alkaline, and not to be deprived of some moisture in summer. Roots are very fibrous, with no rapid or nuisance spread and they can be safely divided in autumn or spring.

The first almost double to be introduced was H. 'Incomparabilis', with its overlapping petals, it has some resemblance to Zinnia. The leaves are oval and saw edged, and the flowering stems very branching to give a bushy type growth by early July, 3 feet high, when the first flowers open. From then on, they come non-stop until well into September.

H. 'Golden Plume' is one of the many new varieties raised by Karl Foerster in Germany, and this too, is almost double flowered at 3½ feet. H. 'Ballerina' is a warm yellow, with less of a double formation and H. *patula* is purely single, as is the taller 4 feet H. *gigantea*. H. 'Goldgreenheart' has a curiously attractive green tinge towards the centre of the otherwise near double flowers of a lighter yellow shade.

Although Heliopsis are amongst the subjects that help to make yellow the predominant colour amongst perennials in late summer, they would be amongst the last I would dispense with in the unlikely event of my deciding to cut down on yellows for I rate them very highly in excellence.

HELLEBORUS ○

HELLEBORUS *orientalis* 'Hybrids'

H. *niger*. There may have been a time—and there may still be a place, for H. niger to live up to its name 'Christmas Rose', but nowadays it scarcely applies. Not that it matters greatly, for it is still the depths of winter when the first white, golden centred flowers appear amid the deep green leaves. It likes a cool root run, neither soggy nor starved and though its preference is for some shade competition with tree roots should be avoided. A light much is helpful, applied in spring and young plants are easier to establish than old. Indeed, divisions of old plants often languish rather than grow. Increase can be made by seed, but this is a slow process. It is usually cheaper to buy young nursery grown plants and having chosen a semi shady place, prepare it well, then after a year or two in which to become firmly established it should then flower year after year, from January to late March. H. *orientalis*: these are much more adaptable and reliable than H. niger. Flowering from February to April, they carry the name 'Lenten Rose'. They come in a colour range, from white, through shades of pink to plum purple, at a time when old leaves, which have been evergreen for 10-11 months have faded. As soon as the flowers begin to fade, then a new crop of leaves, giving a canopy over the roots which helps keep the soil cool in summer. H. orientalis can withstand considerable summer dryness, but what they most prefer is high or dappled shade, or the non-southerly aspect of a wall. They are not fussy about soil, but respond to a light mulch after flowering.

Occasionally named varieties are offered, but these are much more expensive. Old plants can be divided in autumn, though this may spoil flowering for one season, and when planting, roots should go well down, leaving the crown buds only just below ground level. Stems vary in height from 10 to 18 inches but in the deep purple red species, H. *atrorubens* are rather shorter. H. *colchicus* is pink flowered in clusters and apart from flowering sometimes in autumn as well as early spring, has evergreen leaves. H. *corsicus* is also evergreen, but the leaves come from stems which may loll over somewhat and lengthen till a large terminal head of pale apple green flowers open in April. This, and its hybrid H. *sternii* make quite large plants and from seed, take 3 years to flower fully.

HELLEBORUS *niger*

HEUCHERA ○ ◑

HEUCHERA 'Red Spangles'

HEUCHERA 'Greenfinch'

Wherever a garden has well drained soil, Heucheras will flourish and add a unique charm to the early summer scene. They have attractive evergreen foliage which with overlapping and often marbled leaves of rounded ivy shape, is pleasing even when not in flower. In May, the slender stems rise to unfurl with a spike of small bell shaped flowers in a pleasing range of colour, from white to pink, salmon, red and crimson, varying in height from 12 inches to 2½ feet and lasting in flower till well into July. The plants have one fault, despite them being fully hardy and long lived. It is that the crowns above ground gradually extend so that after a few years they become woody and less likely to produce flowers. The remedy is to dig up the plant and pull off some of the crowns which have fibrous roots attached and after preparing the soil again, plant them back more deeply, till only the leafy upper part is above ground and then firm well. This, and any new planting can be done best in late summer or early autumn, but otherwise they are safe enough to move in winter or spring.

The variety H. 'Scintillation' has received the highest possible Awards from the R.H.S. and the red tipped pink bells add much to its brilliance. H. 'Coral Cloud' has smaller flowers on longer stems at 2½ feet with H. 'Firebird' a telling red of 2 feet. H. 'Freedom' is light pink and dwarf only 18 inches high, but both H. 'Greenfinch'—a greenish white and H. 'Hyperion' coral pink, are very strong growing with 2½ feet spikes. H. 'Pearl Drops' has small gracefully carried flowers. H. 'Pretty Polly' is a large flowered clear pink barely 12 inches high. The brightest deep red, with large bells is H. 'Red Spangles' with H. 'Shere Variety' more of a scarlet red, both 2 feet. H. 'Splendour' is outstanding for its glowing salmon scarlet flowers and H. 'Sunset' has coral red lips to deep pink bells.

So much for the named varieties, which can only be increased by division. The best strain of mixed colours from seed is undoubtedly H. 'Bressingham Hybrids' in which the full range of colour is seen.

HEUCHERA ○ ◑

HEUCHERA 'Scintillation'

HEUCHERELLA ◑

HEUCHERELLA 'Bridget Bloom'

This stands for the cross between Heuchera and Tiarella, and it has produced the pretty carpeted H. *tiarelloides*, with golden green foliage 6 inches high and 10-12 inches spikes of light pink in May and June. This is an easy and useful plant, but the cross also yielded H. *'Bridget Bloom'*, a much choicer subject for good light soil and a little shade. The foliage is domed and very compact and where happy it sends up a long succession of flower sprays giving an overall affect of light pink, from individual flowers which contain both white and pink. Quite often this will flower from May to July and again in September or October. It is a plant worth fussing over a little, adding some leafy or peaty soil where heavy and dividing when need be in August-September.

The story behind this plant is worth telling, Percy Piper is on the staff at Bressingham and whether or not tips from me lead him to experiment with crossing different plants he cannot resist 'fiddling' as he calls it with plants that appeal to him. In this case he tried more than once to cross a recently disco-vered species Tiarella wherryi with one of the many improved Heucheras which had al-ready been introduced. For two seasons no seedlings appeared from this artificial bege-neric cross. The third year he tried again by planting one close to the other and from the few seeds which set, fertilised by bees, one plant only appeared next spring and this was it. After that it took 5 years to work up a stock sufficient to offer, since such 'nude' hybrids do not set seed.

Light and shade can be used to full advantage with Perennials. In the shady foreground are Hostas, Astilbe and Rodgersia. Spikey plants intersperse to avoid uniformity. The specimen Conifer in the background is behind another Island Bed, to give winter colour.

HEMEROCALLIS ○ ◑

HEMEROCALLIS *dumortierii*

HEMEROCALLIS 'Stafford'

The Day Lilies have come in for a great deal of attention in recent years from hybridists, both amateur and professional, in both Europe and N. America. The result has naturally been to evolve varieties with larger flowers and to enhance the range of colour, but on the debit side, would be cultivators of them have become bewildered by the proliferation of so many to chose from—which now runs into hundreds and this process is continuing unabated. Several nurserymen carry a stock of a number of varieties and in total there is more than ample range available.

Hemerocallis are very hardy and very adaptable plants, for sun or partial shade and though revelling in rich, fairly moist soil, they will grow and flower where drier conditions prevail, but fall short of the beauty of which they are capable. The rushy leaves of Hemerocallis are fully complementary to the trumpet flowers, coming on smooth stems from 1½ to 3 feet tall. The earliest show colour in May, in the early and dwarf species H. *dumortierii*, which has yellow flowers for several weeks, and another species H. *multiflorus* is orange yellow from June to September in great profusion at 3½ feet.

Those illustrated are all modern varieties and although H. 'Hyperion' was introduced 20 years ago, it is still much in demand for its clear colour and large flowers. A newer and outstanding yellow is H. 'Lark Song'. Other outstanding varieties of proven merit are H. 'Black Magic' deep ruby mahogany, H. 'Contessa', light orange, H. 'Bonanza', soft yellow but very dwarf, matching well with the deeper coloured H. 'Golden Chimes' which is also dwarf. H. 'Golden Orchid' is superb, growing 3 feet, H. 'Nigrette' is mahogany purple, and H. 'Pink Damask' still holds its own as one of the closest to true pink. H. 'Primrose Mascotte', is pale lemon and H. 'Stafford' is an outstanding bronzy red.

Hemerocallis can be planted at any time from early autumn till April. Soil should be enriched in advance, and when fully established some organic fertiliser or mulching in spring will help in producing fine flowers. Plants become large and difficult to lift when old and I have sometimes spaded through a clump in situ either to reduce size or to obtain sections with which to enlarge a group. Such a drastic course has never resulted in causing harm, and is certainly easier than digging up a big plant and then dividing it.

HEMEROCALLIS 'Lark Song'

HEMEROCALLIS 'Mikado'

HEMEROCALLIS 'Imperator'

HEMEROCALLIS 'Pink Damask'

HEMEROCALLIS
'Hyperion'

73

HOSTA

HOSTA 'Thomas Hogg'

HOSTA *fortunei picta*

There is a special value in having plants which have beauty in both flowers and foliage. In this respect, the Hostas of 'Plantain Lilies' are well nigh supreme and it is small wonder that in recent years when foliage effect has become more fully appreciated that they have come in for unprecendented popularity. But for the partiality of some kinds for shade, with soil not lacking in moisture, Hostas have all the qualities one looks for—hardiness and longevity with freedom from trouble as well as beauty and charm. Like several other subjects, the better the treatment given to Hostas—so far as food and drink are concerned, the better the results will be, but many will give a good value even if this aspect is somewhat neglected. They have roots that go a long way down in search of moisture and nutriment, and most of them can stand competition without themselves being agressive. Some have a wide leaf spread and often I have planted a group a several plants 1½ to 2 feet apart only to have to thin them out after 3-4 years growth. As with large clumps of Hemerocallis it is possible to divide them with a sharp spade, but the back to back method with forks will force it asunder with less damage to the fleshy crowns from which growth comes. All die back completely in winter, and leaves unfurl and enlarge in perfect formation ready for the flower spikes which appear from June onwards.

Those with variegated leaves are best in shade and placed away from strong winds as well as strong sun. H. 'Thomas Hogg', is one of the best, and it has lavender mauve flowers on 2½ feet stems, not very different from the wavy edged H. *crispula*, which is rather scarce. H. *sieboldiana elegans* has huge leaves, and of glaucous blue-green and a spread of about 3 feet where well established, with 3 feet spikes of pale lilac white.

HOSTA *undulata medio-variegata*

HOSTA

HOSTA *sieboldiana elegans*

HOSTA *crispula*

H. *glauca* is similar but smaller and H. *glauca coerula* has rounded, ribbed leaves that come closest to blue of any. H. *fortunei* itself is glaucous leaved and has mauve-lilac flowers in June-July. Its form H. *fortunei picta*, comes with vernal leaves showing a bright yellowish flush, from April to June, when on flowering the leaves turn green. There is a golden variegated edged form H. *fortunei aurea marginata* and also a golden foliage form H. *fortunei aurea*, although the leaves turn a light green as spring turns to summer. H. *ventricosa* flowers very freely, lavender coloured on 3 feet spikes above handsome foliage, and H. *ventricosa variegata* has similar flowers but rich green leaves that are so decked with yellow variegation as to make it one of the finest of all variegated Hostas. H. *rectifolia*, is green leaved with a profusion of upstanding purple flower spikes to 4 feet to make an imposing sight in July and August.

The variety H. 'Honeybells' has lavender mauve flowers above green leaves and these have the added attraction of being perfumed. H. *undulata erromena* is one of the most adaptable, the leaves being green with a wavy edge. This wave is more pronounced in H. *undulata medio variegata*, which is much smaller in leaf and only 18 inches in flower, but the foliage remains bright throughout the summer. H. *lancifolia* is neat growing, and its green spear shaped leaves overlap in perfect mounded formation, with deep mauve flowers coming on 2 feet stems in August and September. H. *plantaginea* is late flowering, but some find it shy in this respect, having planted in a shady place along with other Hostas. This is a mistake for although it grows best in shade and moisture, it needs sun and warmth to induce the charming scented white flowers to appear on their 2½ feet spikes. H. *plantaginea grandiflora* is the best one to go for. Another white is the midget H. *minor alba* which barely reaches 12 inches high and has green leaves. It flowers in July-August, but another dwarf, the choice H. *tardiflora has* mauve purple flowers in early autumn.

INCARVILLEA ○

INULA ○

INCARVILLEA *delavayi*

At first sight, the exotic looking rosy red trumpets of these seem out of place amongst hardy perennials. They have some resemblance to Gloxineas, and since they appear rather suddenly from bare earth, before making leaf, they are all the more startling. The roots are in fact fleshy fangs, and though no sign of shoots may be visible at the beginning of May, by the end of the month they are showing bud if not actually in flower. I. *delavayi*, is the taller of the species available and gradually run up with dark green deeply cut leaves, flowering all through June, till they reach 2 feet or so. I. *grandiflora*, which has the larger trumpets of deep pinkish red, begins flowering only just above ground in late May, and when fully grown, is no more than 12 inches high. It has a similar fleshy root and though these plants are both fully hardy they need well drained soil to be long lived and care with cultivating tools during their winter dormancy. Roots are difficult to divide and they can be increased only by seed.

With the common name of 'Fleabane', Inulas may have little herbal value nowadays, but there are a few that merit a place for the show of yellow, finely rayed flowers they produce. All are easy to grow in ordinary soil and all respond to division in autumn or spring. I. *orientalis* has large flowers 3-4 inches across delicately rayed for all its lack of height. It grows to 20 inches but lacks also a long flowering period, covering 3-4 weeks only in June-July. I. *ensifolia compacta* by comparison, flowers on and on, from late June to September, with 1 inch yellow flowers on bushy growth only 9 inches high. At more than twice the height, up to 2 feet, I. *'Golden Beauty'* has a similar long period in flower and a bushy habit, but I. *hookeri* is rather floppy. This has soft green leaves and on this dense mass of greenery it makes 2-2½ feet high, comes a long succession of rayed yellow daisies from June onwards. Plants spread quite quickly and may need curbing after 2 years, but I. *magnifica* needs space for its big clock-like foliage which spreads out from a compact but hefty deep rooted rootstock. Stems grow massively to 5 or 6 feet branching above with yellow flowers 3-4 inches across from June to August.

INULA *orientalis*

HYLOMECON ◑

HYLOMECON *japonicum* (syn *vernalis*)

H. *vernalis* (syn. japonicum), is a delightful member of the Poppy family for spring flowering, best in light or humus soil and a little shade for preference. It spreads with slow growing matted roots and shoots below ground, and has light green foliage appearing in March, to form good ground cover and in this, the yellow cups flower in April and May. This is a plant that responds either to division and replanting every 3-4 years, or to an annual mulch of peat or compost in autumn, since it has a tendency to become too congested and has no deep penetration of roots, division is a very simple matter, but best done in autumn.

The above picture gives some idea of the range of colours to be found in varieties of *Iris germanica* or 'Flag Iris'

IRIS *germanica* 'Wabash'

IRIS

What was said of the bewildering range of Hemerocallis varieties applies equally if not more so to Iris, especially the *germanica* or 'June flowering'. Every conceivable combination of colours, in which blue, white, purple, yellow or brown-red are basic, exists somewhere or other as a named variety. The upstanding portion of the flower, known as the 'Standard' and the drooping tongue like petal known as 'Falls' are often of differing colours, and it can only be a matter of choice from seeing them in flower, or as colour illustrations, that one can make a choice on which appeals most to individual taste. A list of recommendations from the use of words would be quite inadequate to say the least, because some with several colours merging on the same flowers are virtually beyond accurate description within the limits of space such a book as this imposes. The June flowering Iris need sun and good drainage but have no liking for rich soil or manure, other than a lime or phosphatic

IRIS

A further selection of *Iris germanica*

IRIS *pallida variegata*

IRIS *pallida variegata*

based fertiliser. Planting is best in July-September and when dividing for replanting, discard the centre parts of an old clump. The rhizome should not be buried entirely, only barely below surface, but the fibrous root at the base of each fan should be well down and well spread.

I. *pumila* is a miniature race, flowering April-May from 6-10 inches high in blue, purple, yellow and white. I. *sibirica* grows rushily to 3-4 feet from a plant that becomes quite large in the moist soil these prefer. They flower under various names, in blue, white and deep purple shades, and though flowers are small, they make quite a show in June-July in the right place. I. *kaempferi* have large, wide open flowers up to 5 inches across. These dislike excessive winter wet, excessive summer dryness and alkalinity of soil, but where they grow well, they are a real joy. Heights are about 2½-3 feet and colours range from snow white through many shades of blue and purple. These, and the sibiricas are best divided in spring. Two variegated leaved Iris are worth mentioning I. *pallida variegata* has blue flowers in June, and a year round leafage, with glaucous grey-green strongly marked primrose yellow. These prefer sun, with ordinary soil, but I. *foetidissima variegata* is best in quite deep shade, and does not object to dry soil. The leaves are deep green, streaked and shiny with light yellow, and though flowers are of no account one sometimes sees bright red seeds as pods burst open.

IRIS

IRIS *pumila*

IRIS
germanica
'Golden Fleece'

IRIS *kaempferi*

IRIS *sibirica*

KNIPHOFIA

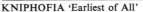

KNIPHOFIA 'Brimstone'   KNIPHOFIA 'Earliest of All'   KNIPHOFIA 'Bee's Sunset'

Not all 'Red Hot Pokers' are of that colour, for nowadays there is white, yellow and many shades between, as well as red. But the one thing they have in common, though some are only 18 inches high and others a massive 6 feet, is the need for good drainage. Their roots penetrate to a great depth to find all they need even in poor soil and indeed I have known plants to be killed by kindness by applying manure or compost in the hope of feeding them well. They also prefer to be left alone for several years at a stretch and if planting or dividing, one must be careful to avoid roots becoming dry through exposure, and by making a good deep hole so they do not lay bent or bunched after insertion. Spring is much the best time for moving Kniphofias, but it is safe enough for any that have flowered to plant in August or September. For large old plants the back to back method using two forks is best, trying as best one can to avoid damage to the fleshy parts between leaf and root. In some very cold districts

or where soil becomes sticky in winter, a collar of litter around plants, after tying up the leaves, is good practice. The effect of the former is to keep the soil and roots from freezing and the latter a precaution against slush and damp entering the crowns which might freeze or set up a rotting process. Having an overall stately appearance, the taller growing kinds especially, are best in some isolation, using a very much dwarfer subject if need be in front so as not to detract.

The first Kniphofias flower in June with, K 'Gold Else', a pure yellow, 3 feet high, and K. 'Atlanta'. This has very broad leaves and is robust in every way, with heavy red and yellow pokers 3½ feet. K. 'Earliest of All' is not quite accurate, but at least it is the earliest of these with flame-red spikes. Also early are two new grassy leaved and slender spiked varieties—K. 'Bressingham Flame', deep orange and K. 'Bressingham Torch', orange flame,

KNIPHOFIA

KNIPHOFIA 'Bressingham Flame'

both erect and graceful at 3 feet. K. *tubergenii* is primrose yellow, 3 feet and K. '*Bees Sunset*' a glowing orange of similar height. For July-August there is the deep orange K. '*Ada*' 3½ feet. K. '*Maid of Orleans*' white, tinged pink, K. '*Jenny Bloom*' salmon-peach— a most unusual shade, and K. '*Modesta*', a dwarf, rosette leaved ivory suffused pink only 2 feet high. K. '*Springtime*' is robust at 4 feet with orange red tipped flowers and the fiery red K. '*Samuel's Sensation*' has 5 feet spikes in August-September. K. '*Brimstone*' is a late flowering canary yellow, 3½ feet high, but the rare K. *galpinii* flowers in October with dainty 20 inches orange spikes.

Mixed colours from seed are of course the cheapest to buy, but whatever one decides to grow, a useful hint is to remove faded spikes, for this will prolong the flowering period or encourage them to throw a second crop in the case of early flowering varieties.

Another section of a bed which emphasises the striking spikey plants. *Lythrum 'Rose Queen'* flowers for weeks, and the yellow spikes of *Ligularia 'The Rocket'* are very striking. In the foreground, *Trollius* gave their display some weeks earlier.

Many Perennials can be used in such arrangements as this for winter decoration.

Left

Island Bed formation by grouping and grading for height pays dividends. The frontal group is *Stokesia 'Blue Star'* which flowers on and on.

Centre

A vista of perennials is another of the informal settings at Bressingham. The Phlox in the foreground is *'Starfire'*, the brightest red with the best constitution.

Left

Broad grass paths give and ideal setting for perennials. In the foreground is the dwarf double *Gypsohila compacta plena*.

LIGULARIA ○ ◑
(see also Senecio)

These are imposing subjects for rich or moist soil, though the L. *clivorum* varieties need considerable space in which to develop. This makes a large leaved clump and sends up erect spikes to 3 or 4 feet of orange yellow daisy flowers, and the variety L. '*Desdemona*', has handsome purplish leaves. Flowering time is July-August, but L. *hodgsoni* is dwarfer and earlier at 2½ feet though on similar lines. L. *stenocephala* is tall and handsome with light yellow flowers. Several other species exist, more suited perhaps to wet or bog garden conditions. All can be increased by division in autumn or spring, but show the effects of droughty conditions rather quickly if deprived of moisture during the growing period, and this is one of the reasons why ample space should be given them when planting.

LIGULARIA *clivorum*

LIGULARIA *stenocephala*

LAMIUM ○ ◑ ●

LAMIUM *maculatum* 'Chequers'

The main virtue of L. *maculatum* and L. *galeobdolon* is that they will grow in shade, even if dry. The former makes a rapid spread 6 inches or so above ground with deadnettle leaves which are heavily spotted a paler grey-green. The flowers come on 8-9 inches stumpy spikes in spring, in white, purplish and pink, and L. '*Chequers*' is about the most colourful and compact variety. L. *galeobdolon variegatum* spreads quickly from runners and the leaves are in a bicolor variegation. Flowers are yellow in May, soon over, but in general these are easy plants for the more difficult places. L. *garganicum* is much more choice, making a compact evergreen mound of light green and a long succession of deep pink flowers. Whilst L. *orvala* has erect spikes almost 2 feet high in May-June, deep pink in colour and quite showy, but dying away to a dormant slow growing root in winter. These last two species need shade, in soil that does not dry out but can be increased by division.

LIATRIS ○

'Gay Feather' is a good name for this showy plant. Though easy to grow in any well drained soil, it has a fleshy root with no deep penetration and responds to being divided or replanted every 3-4 years, because of its tendency to grow out of the ground. Deep green narrow leaves furnish both the plant and the stems which rise up to 3 feet and by late June, the fluffy little flowers, close to the stem open first at the top. This is the opposite to most spike forming plants, but as flowering proceeds downwards, fading does not seriously detract from what is a quite striking appearance. Cutting back when faded, often induces further spikes to flower into August and September, but division is best in spring. Though several species exist, L. *callilepis* has been found to be the most reliable of these, such as L. *spicata* and L. *pychnostachya* which are on similar lines.

LIATRIS *callilepis*

LIRIOPE ○ ◐

LIRIOPE *muscari*

Given lime free or neutral soil, this is a sterling long lived plant for either sun or shade. In the species L. *muscari*, the plants grow into quite hefty tufts, with abundant evergreen bladed leaves of dark shiny green, to about 15 inches high and just above nestle small spikes of bright lilac blue flowers in late summer and autumn. Individual flowers are small, reminiscent as the specific name denotes, of the 'Grape Hyacinth'. The roots are a mass of fibre plus storage nodules and plants can withstand drought, flowering best in sunny conditions. L. *'Majestic'* will not flower except in a very sunny place. It is dwarfer and broader leaved, but flowers are larger in a deep lavender blue. Both can be divided in spring, and being slow to recover, should be left alone as long as possible. L. muscari is a subject of such adaptability and usefulness that is should be more widely grown.

LUPIN ○ ◑

Virtually all Lupins nowadays originate from the Russell strain. They are so easy from seed that many people prefer this cheaper method, whether they sow their own or buy in seedling plants. One should bear in mind however, that from seed, there are reversionary tendencies and to obtain the best spikes and colours, seed must be carefully chosen. Mixed colours are of course inevitable from seed and named varieties to colour are more expensive because they can only be increased from basal cuttings in early spring. Ample variety exists in nurserymen's catalogues for those who wish to make their own selection of colours, and though new varieties appear fairly regularly, it is often a case of trial, since some are constitutionally stronger and more perennial than others. Lupins are not so happy on limey soils as in acid or neutral or low alkalinity. They dislike humus rich soils too, and should not receive compost or manure, and if they cannot be regarded as long lived perennials, they are at least adaptable for open as well as shady conditions and town gardens.

LUPIN 'Russell Hybrids'

LYCHNIS

LYCHNIS *chalcedonica*

LYCHNIS *viscaria splendens plena*

LYCHNIS *coronaria*

Several of the 'Campions' are good garden plants needing no fussing, but varying considerably from species to species. L. *arkwrightii* for instance has a very puny root, but quite large heads of brilliant scarlet vermilion flowers on 12 inches purple leaved stems. It will come from seed and lives only 2-3 years. L. *chalcedonica* however, will reach 3 feet in good soil, with leafy stems and topped with a close head of small scarlet flowers. This is longer lived and will divide, as will the tufty L. *viscaria splendens plena*, which makes a bright display of double deep pink carnation like flowers in June-July, only 10 inches high. There is a pretty single white form of L. *viscaria*, which is a little taller and longer flowering but for long flowering L. *coronaria* is excellent. It makes a mound of soft silvery foliage and loose branching sprays of pink or red flowers. Though not a long living plant it comes easily from seed. L. *cognata* is a rarer species with rich red flowers on bushy 12 inches growth.

LYSIMACHIA ○ ◐

These are easy to grow plants in any but dry situations, or perhaps it should be said that they grow and flower more freely where not dry. L. *clethroides* grows from a mat of closely packed creeping shoots and from each rises an erect leafy stem to about 4 feet in good soil. In late summer this opens as a spike of small white flowers, curiously but attractively angled and curved. A tendency for stems to become starved through overcrowding can be overcome by digging a portion of an old clump with some compost. L. *punctata* has a more vigorous spread below ground, and where moist, these may need curbing. This is the 'Yellow Loosestrife' and very attractive it is with its leaf packed stems and whorls of bright yellow flowers from midsummer onwards for several weeks, growing to 2½ to 3 feet. A more statuesque species with a compact root exists in L. *ephemerum*. The leaves are pointed oval, smooth and shiny and from June to August come tapering spikes up to 4 feet of white flowers. Unlike the others, this does not readily divide and is not so constitutionally strong and adaptable.

LYSIMACHIA *clethroides*

LYTHRUM ○ ◐

One of the most adaptable of all hardy plants, these will grow in damp or waterside situations, or in quite ordinary soil even if on the dry side. The roots are tough and woody and will not divide until plants become quite old In any case they can be left to take care of themselves for years, and form erect, twiggy bushes. Varieties of L. *salicaria* are quite leafy, with profuse but small spikes of intense rose red in the variety L. *'Firecandle'*. L. *'The Beacon'* is a little less deep in colour, and both form bushes 3 feet tall, flowering from June to late August. L. *'Robert'* grows only 2 feet with spikes of bright pink. L. *virgatum* has less foliage and more slender spikes and flowers a little later of which L. *'Rose Queen'* is a favourite pink variety, 1½ to 2 feet high.

LYTHRUM *salicaria* 'Firecandle'

MACLEAYA ○ ◐

MACLEAYA *cordifolia*

M. *cordifolia*, is an excellent background subject—whether used at the rear of dwarfer kinds, or against a background of evergreens, or a building. The leaves are an attractive bronzy green and stems are strong. Flowers may be small, but make a very pleasing cut flower. The roots are somewhat fleshy and have the capacity for a fairly rapid spread in light soil, appearing some distance from the original plant. Such new growth can be hoed off or dug out if not wanted, because otherwise plants can be left alone for several years to give a distinctive display from their 5 feet spikes in August-September. This is the true species, but what is sometimes offered as M. *cordifolia 'Coral Plume'*, is in fact a clone of M. *microcarpa*. This has very tiny flowers indeed, presenting a hazy coral brown effect on spikes 6 feet or more high and the same handsome foliage. It has the same kind of root system—easy to increase, long lived and adaptable.

MONARDA ○ ◐

The curiously shaped flowers of the Bergamot have a certain appeal, and the leaves are decidedly aromatic even if this does not appeal to everyone. They come in some very bright colours, on erectly branching stems up to 4 feet in moist or rich soil, but less than this where dry. The plants make a fairly rapid spread of matted rooting pieces and these may need curbing. This is easy enough since they almost fall apart, and with their tendency to wander, one simple method is to dig in the centre parts with a little compost and to plant again some of the vigorous outer pieces in spring. M. *'Adam'* is cerise red, and M. *'Cambridge Scarlet'* is still popular along with M. *'Croftway Pink'*, M. *'Prairie Glow'*, is bright salmon red, and M. *'Prairie Night'* is violet purple, all growing to a similar height. Monardas are however capable of growing quite tall in the second year after planting, in rich or moist soil.

MONARDA 'Croftway Pink'

MONARDA 'Cambridge Scarlet'

NEPETA ○ ◑

Though 'Catmint' is one of the commonest of dwarf hardy plants it remains one of the most widely used. The correct name is reckoned now to be N. *faasenii*, but as it is too well known as N. *mussinii*, is never likely to be accepted. The constant demand for this plant is due to its habit of dying out in winter through wetness. In dry places it will survive on poor soils, to give successive displays, but it does improve for being divided into quite small pieces every 2-3 years. N. mussinii grows about 12 inches and flowers from June to September, but the taller N. *'Six Hills'*, with stems about 2 feet, is less neat and tidy. An uncommon variety with much larger flowers exists in N. *grandiflora 'Blue Beauty'*. This has erect spikes of lavender blue flowers, 18-20 inches high from June to August, but the roots are rather rampant below ground and replanting every 2-3 years is advised. All three Nepetas are best planted or divided in spring and division of N. mussinii in autumn may well prove a fatal mistake.

NEPETA *mussinii*

NERINE ○ ◑

N. *bowdenii*. Not many bulbs come within the scope of the book on hardy perennials, but this autumn flowering beauty must be one of the exceptions. It is a subject that needs the shelter of a wall or shrubs other than north facing, and once established, bulbs will increase naturally and no matter how congested they become, they will make a bright show just before the onset of winter in October and November. Stems are 15-18 inches high, and they last well in water. Fresh plantings should be covered with some protective litter until new leaves appear in spring, as bulbs should be set only just below surface. Leaves die off in late summer just before flowering begins.

NERINE *bowdenii*

Here are Perennials revelling in moisture. The noble plumes of *Aruncus*, keep company with *Astilbe 'Bressingham Beauty'*, in front and not yet flowering, the variegated *Iris kaempferi*, and in front a Marsh Marigold *(Caltha)* has already flowered.

OENOTHERA ○

The name 'Evening Primrose' applies to O. *biennis* and not to the perennial kinds mentioned below, though all have the same tendency to open their flowers at eventide. O. *missouriensis*, makes a wide summer surface spread, dense with glaucous leaves and from July to September, nestle large canary yellow cups of great beauty. The root is fangy and not very large considering the amount of growth and it is a better subject for a sunny bank than amongst other more upright perennials. O. *'Fireworks'* makes a more compact plant with colourful leaves in spring and twiggy stems to 1½ feet carrying bright yellow flowers from June to August. O. *cinaeus*, is very similar though vernal foliage is even more colourful. There are several other yellows, of similar neat clumpy habit, all very showy, with flowers 2 inches or more across, during the same period. O. *'Yellow River'* grows to about 18 inches, but O. *'Highlight'* is 2 feet, flowering with great profusion but sometimes needing supports. O. missouriensis can only be increased by seed, but for the rest, spring division is best and any good garden soil suits them.

OENOTHERA *missouriensis*

OENOTHERA 'Fireworks'

OPHIOPOGON *planiscarpus nigrescens*

OPHIOPOGON ◐ ●

O. *planiscapus nigrescens* has the appearance of a grass, but it is in fact a member of the Lily family, related to Liriope. Growth is unfortunately slow and though hardy and long lived, it is not happy in poor soils and dry sunny places. Its dark, almost black leaves seldom fail to appeal and though it flowers in late summer, in the form of 4 inches spikes of little heads, these are not very distinguished. The plain green O. *planiscapus* is only slightly more vigorous and though both take a year or two to become established, they can in course of time be divided, best in spring.

PACHYSANDRA

PACHYSANDRA *terminalis*

P. *terminalis* is inserted because it is the kind of plant many gardeners need of something to grow near or beneath trees. It is of evergreen sub-shrubby growth, giving permanent and trouble free ground cover and able to compete with the roots of trees and shrubs once established. It is especially useful as a ground cover between shrubs and has a slow, sure spread. The type is green leaved but P. *terminalis variegata* is brighter. Both have flowers of rather nondescript appearance, which neither add nor detract. Both can be divided safely in spring, since their spread is a case of rooting as they go.

Though this is undoubtedly one of the best evergreen ground coverers, able to fill spaces in many an otherwise inhospitably shady place, it is rather slow to become established. In the first year plants take hold, but show little spread. If planted 12 inches apart, they should meet to become a complete carpet, touching each other in 2-3 years and if after that one wishes to extend the area, rooted pieces can be taken out without being missed.

OMPHALODES

OMPHALODES *cappadocica* 'Anthea Bloom'

O. *cappadocica* is a charming, reliable little plant for shady places, making a thick carpet of semi-glaucous ribbed leaves, evergreen for most of the year. In April-May come little 8 inches sprays of intensely blue forget-me-not type flowers above the foliage and the variety O. 'Anthea Bloom' is sky blue and freest to flower. There is nothing weedy about this plant and though it can stand summer drought an occasional dusting of fine soil or peat amongst the leaves in autumn, will help it maintain its carpeting qualities and improve its flowering. Early autumn is the best time for dividing or planting and once settled it should be allowed to stay down for several years.

O. *verna* grows much more quickly, rooting as it goes. It makes quite a show, with bright blue flowers on 3 inches sprays in May though it does not flower for long. The leaves are bright green, but these fade in autumn. There is a white flowered form of this and in both cases a soil dusting during winter is helpful, otherwise it is a good tempered subject for shady places

PAEONIA *festiva maxima*

PAEONIA *mlokosewitschii*

PAEONIA ○

A very old clump of Paeonia

Paeonies are amongst the longest lived of plants, and should be planted for permanence, because they prefer to be left alone—for fifty years if need be and because of this a site should be carefully chosen. Paeonies need an open situation and good deep soil—regardless of texture or alkalinity. They do in fact like lime, and flower best if given top dressing of fertiliser in late summer or early autumn when new feeding roots begin again. This too, is the best planting time, and nursery grown plants—not newly cut up divisions will give best results. Paeonies can be divided but it calls for skill with a knife and one should not expect flowers in its first season. Planting depth is important. The pinkish crown buds on which next seasons growth depends should be settled at no more than one inch below surface after firming round the plant.

The largest flowered Paeonies are the P. *lactiflora* varieties which flower in June. These are mostly doubles of which P. *festiva maxima*. P. *'Sarah Bernhardt'*, and others illustrated are good examples. A vast range of varieties exists, apart from those basic colours of red, pink and white, some having merging shades and others with a deeper base. There are some fine single and semi double varieties in this range also of which P. *'King Arthur'* is a good example, with its gold centre on a dark red background. P. *'Bowl of Beauty'* has huge flowers of rose pink in which the

PAEONIA 'Sarah Bernhardt'

PAEONIA ○

creamy centre stands out, and P. *'Defender'* has massive blood red flowers. Some white varieties shade towards creamy yellow in the centre, but the self coloured single P. *mlokosewitschii* is a glistening colour. This is a much sought after plant despite its difficult name, not only because of its colour but because it flowers in April-May, before any others.

Other earlier Paeonies include the limited range of P. *officinalis*—mostly doubles in pink, white and red, flowering in May at 3 feet. Then there are one or two brilliant P. *lobata* varieties, single salmon red in the 2 feet high P. *'Sunshine'*, and the single red P. *smouthii* and the deep pink P. *arietina* are charming. Well grown plants of Paeonies may be more expensive to buy, but when one considers the returns over a period of many years, then they become a very good investment.

PAEONIA off. rubra plena

PAEONIA 'Kelway's Lovely'   PAEONIA 'King Arthur

PAPAVER

PAPAVER *orientalis* 'Goliath'

Oriental Poppies are amongst the most gorgeous of perennial flowers. Some varieties often fail to reach perfection because the flowers are too heavy for the stems, but P. '*Goliath*' is not one of these, for it always stands unaided and with such richness of colour is a focal point in the garden from late May to early July. Other upstanding varieties are the scarlet P. '*Marcus Perry*' and P. '*Perry's White*'. These all grow to 3 feet and there are slightly shorter ones in the single pink P. '*Mrs. Perry*', and P. '*Stormtoch*' orange red, and P. '*Indian Chief*' brownish red, whilst P. '*Snowflame*' has an unusual suffusion of orange, red and white.

Papavers have deep fleshy roots and will not only increase from root cuttings, but an old plant being dug up, will shoot from roots left behind. The long, roughly hairy leaves are lush in spring, but unless plants are cut back after flowering, they look untidy. Cutting back induces a fresh crop of leaves to help cover what might otherwise be more or less bare ground. Poor, rather than rich soil is best for these Poppies, since richness makes for over tall weak growth and wetness may result in winter losses through crown rot.

POLYGONATUM *multiflorum*

POLYGONATUM

This is best known as 'Solomon's Seal', a plant for cool shady positions or a wild-garden, rather than in an open bed or border. The crowns form a mat just below the surface and though it takes a year or so for new plantings to settle down, once established they spread slowly but surely and need no more attention, given reasonably good soil, not too dry. The most usual Solomon's Seal grown is the free flowering P. *multiflorum*, but P. *japonicum* has larger leaves and flowers, and is a little taller at 3 feet. There is a variegated leaved form of the latter which is rather scarce. Autumn is the best time to move or plant Polygonatums, and it pays to give them a good start preparing a place within the influence of tree roots by thorough digging, adding compost, manure or peat.

This too is an Island Bed, for there is another path behind in front of the evergreen background. To the left is the cheerful *Alchemilla mollis*, and the tall white *Campanula lactiflora alba*.

PENSTEMON ○ ◑

The variety P. 'Garnet' has proved to be the hardiest of a genus, which but for their unreliability under our climate conditions, would rank highly. P. 'Garnet' is one of several varieties of P. *hartwegii*, some of which are popular for summer bedding—such as P. 'Southgate Gem' a large flowered pink. They grow to about 2½ feet in bushy formation from a somewhat woody rootstock, and have narrow shiny green leaves. Young plants can be produced from cuttings taken in autumn under glass or in spring from basal shoots and flowering lasts from July to October. A brighter red than P. Garnet exists in P. 'Firebird', though this is not quite so hardy, but the smaller flowered P. 'Pink Endurance' is so far living up to its name. This has a more slender habit and grows to about 2 feet. Penstemons are not fussy about soil, but they must have good drainage. A very strong point with the above Penstemons is their ability to flower on and on, and young plants, whether nursery grown or not, which have been reared from cuttings taken the previous autumn will bush out and begin flowering by July. From then until autumn they are always in flower, especially if finished spikes are removed. There are incidentally scores of species in existence, some of which are worth trying. P. *digitaloides* is fairly reliable and as the name denotes is rather like a Foxglove in habit. A new hybrid P. *fruticosus* 'Katherine de la Mere' is semi shrubby, with lilac pink spikes 18 inches high, June to September and this holds the promise of being hardy.

PHLOX

PHLOX *paniculata* 'Vintage Wine'

These can make an immense contribution towards colourful gardens in late summer, at a time when yellows would otherwise predominate. Every shade of pink, red, purple, lavender blue, as well as white and orange scarlet is met in the vast number of varieties now in existence, and by judicious planning for colour effect, using Phlox between other subjects perfection in contrasts can be obtained. They prefer good light soil and are least happy on alkaline clay, though in this they respond to the addition of peat, sand or compost. They also respond to mulching in winter so that their feeding roots can benefit and a better summer display will ensue. Nursery grown plants from root cuttings will invariably do better than divisions, because the one pest which sometimes affects them—eelworm—is a risk either from division or tip cuttings.

PHLOX

PHLOX *paniculata* 'Admiral'

Heights of Phlox, as well as times of flowering vary a little with season or climate conditions. Naturally they grow taller given ample moisture and where dry and sunny, they are dwarfer and earlier to flower. An average height is 3 feet and usually they first show colour by mid July, the peak month is August. Young plants produce the largest flower heads, and when plants become old, it improves the quality of flowers by thinning out a congestion of flowering stems during May or June.

Apart from P. 'Harlequin' which has attractive variegated foliage the P. *maculata* species make a change from the more usual form. This grows from a more matted type of plant—very responsive to feeding and the stems carry heads of more columnar shape, with narrow pointed leaves. The range of colour limited to the clear pink of P. 'Alpha' and the white, purple eyed P. 'Omega', both of which flower for a long time from late June, and both attaining 2½-3 feet.

PHLOX 'Harlequin'

Badly affected plants should be dug up and burned and it is not safe to replant on the same spot with Phlox for at least 3 years. Symptoms are shrivelled and distorted stems during the growing period.

Phlox can be planted at any time after September up to late April and their fibrous roots should be well spread in freshly dug and enriched soil, spaced at about 18 inches apart. Those illustrated are all varieties of proven merit, but do not of course cover the whole range of colours. P. 'Balmoral' is a rosy lavender. P. 'Brigadier', orange scarlet. P. 'Endurance', salmon orange. P. 'Gaiety', cherry red. P. 'Hampton Court', amethyst blue. P. 'Dodo Hanbury Forbes', large pink. P. 'July Glow', an early red. P. 'Marlborough' purple with dark foliage. P. 'Mia Ruys', dwarf white. P. 'Red Indian' deep crimson. P. 'Tenor' early scarlet. P. 'The King', late violet purple; P. 'Toits de Paris' light lavender and white. P. 'Admiral' an excellent taller white.

PHLOX

PHLOX *maculata* 'Alpha'

PHLOX

PHLOX *paniculata* 'Starfire'

PHLOX *paniculata* 'Mother of Pearl'

PHLOX *paniculata* 'Sandringham'

PHLOX *paniculata* 'Prince of Orange'

PHYSALIS *franchettii*

PHYSALIS ○

P. *franchettii*, whilst in summer growth makes little display. Leafy, bushy growth and rather nondescript white flowers. But once the leaves begin to fade in autumn, then is revealed the extraordinary bags enclosing a small orange fruit, to give it the name 'Chinese Lantern'. Stems can be cut and used for winter decoration. Plants are very easy growing in any soil, but they wander below ground rather agressively. Because of this they are best rounded up every year or two and placed back into position, if grown in a mixed bed or border, but better still, grown in some spot on their own, purely for cutting. Though invasive by nature, this plant responds to good treatment and a light annual mulch after forking out any over congestion of the matted roots which run just below the surface, will quickly restore full vitality and produce much longer, stronger stems. Where a small patch or row is down for cutting, this would need doing every 2-3 years. The time to cut Physalis is when the leaves begin to fade, for it is then that the 'lanterns' begin to take their colourful tint. Stems should be cut close to the ground and by tying up a few in a bunch and hanging them upside down in a dry airy place, the colouring and drying process will complete itself. After a few weeks they can then be brought indoors to stand in a vase without water, or used in a variety of ways for winter decoration, one of which is to open the lanterns.

PHYSOSTEGIA 'Vivid'

PHYSOSTEGIA ○ ◑

The variety P. *'Vivid'* is the latest to flower—in September, the 12-18 inches spikes coming from quick spreading underground shoots and which need curbing, or setting back into position in spring. P. *'Rose Bouquet'* grows 2½ feet and is lilac pink, July-September, when the 3 feet deep pink spikes of P. *'Summer Spire'* taper up to flower on slender spikes. These two, and the pretty white P. *'Summer Snow'* also 3 feet are less rampant than P. *'Vivid'*, but grow with vigour in any ordinary soil. They are easily divided in spring. The name 'Obedient Plant' comes from the fact that when the little tubular flowers arranged in rows on the spike, are pushed aside, they stay put without snapping off or springing back.

Plants which are easy to grow cannot often be termed distinctive, but this is true of Physostegia. Spike forming plants are moreover very helpful in breaking up any tendency to uniformity in a border or bed, and these with their long flowering habit, fill such a need. They are however subjects that thrive in good soil which does not dry out severely and though this produces fuller, taller spikes, it also involves the need, after a year or two, to thin out some of their roots or to replant.

PLATYCODON ○ ◑

The name 'Balloon Flower' comes from the way in which the petals are joined to form a bag, until they finally open and if pinched just previously, they pop. When open, the flowers are saucer shaped and make a good show for a long time. Roots are fleshy, easy to grow in any well drained soil, but shoots are rather late to appear in spring. Old plants can be divided in spring. P. *grandiflorum* grows to 1½ to 2 feet in white and pale blue. The semi double P. *'Snowflake'* is a first class plant, as is the pale pink P. *'Mother of Pearl'*. P. *mariesii* grows only 12-18 inches and the colour whilst mainly blue, varies slightly from mid to light blue, with a flowering period of several weeks from mid June onwards-and no fads. There is a fairly new oriental species named P. *apoyana* which was hailed as something outstanding because it was dwarf, large flowered and deep coloured. I found however that it was not outstanding and having raised some from seed, it showed much the same height. These are all good garden plants but to my mind the semi double white P. *'Snowflakes'* is the most attractive, for there is no tendency, at 2 feet tall for it being overlooked or to become tarnished by being too lax and dwarf.

PLATYCODON *mariesii*

POLEMONIUM ○ ◑

The old fashioned 'Jacobs Ladder', P. *coeruleum* is short lived and can be a nuisance from self seeding. P. *foliosissimum* is long lived and very long flowering with no nuisance value. The lavender blue flowers come in heads above 2½ feet erect and leafy plants and have been known to remain in flower from late May to September. Polemoniums are not fussy as to soil and there are two dwarf May-June flowering varieties in P. *'Blue Pearl'* and P. *'Sapphire'*, the latter being the taller at 18 inches. P. *'Pink Beauty'* is slightly bronzy leaved and has pinkish mauve flowers on low bushy growth, 15 inches high from June to August. Polemoniums have fibrous roots and are easy to divide in spring.

The need to divide comes once the plant is seen to be producing fewer flowers though the clump has become large and inclined to sit on the ground rather than being in it at the original depth. This applies less to P. *foliosissimum'* than to the others, which may well need dividing and replanting more deeply after about three years. There are several clump forming subjects which tend to grow out of the ground when they become old and it is a matter of observation when this needs doing, with the symptoms mentioned above in mind.

POLEMONIUM *foliosissimum*

POLYGONUM ○ ◑

This vast genus includes some vigorous and even weedy species, but some slow growing varieties as well, along with a range of good, easy garden worthy subjects. P. *amplexicaule* makes a massive leafy bush to 4-5 feet, on which from July to September come countless little spikes of ruby red in the variety P. *atrosanguineum* and scarlet in P. *'Firetail'*. Plants grow into large clumps but should be divided in spring only. P. *bistorta superbum* grows fairly quickly where moist and in May-June sends up 3 feet poker spikes of clear pink. P. *carneum* has smaller deep pink pokers, but grows more compactly, flowering in June-July. The *affine* varieties are useful carpeters, having a fairly rapid surface spread, green in summer, brown in winter. The 9 inches spikes of P. *'Darjeeling Red'* are in fact deep pink, coming in autumn, but P. *'Donald Lowndes'* are bright pink and more showy though no taller. These come on and off all summer and both plants are useful amongst shrubs, on banks, or in frontal positions. P. *viviparum album* is not pure white, but has erect pokers to 15 inches high, capable of making seed which germinates before it drops.

The following Polygonums are choice, but well worth some extra trouble, P. *miletti*, given moist humus soil and some shade will throw up a long succession of deep red pokers on 15 inches stems, beginning in June.

P. *sphaerostachyum* makes a dense bushy spread above ground, though the first deep pink spikes begin in late May, soon after new growth begins. From then on flowering is virtually non stop till September making a very bright show indeed. P. sphaerostachyum likes it fairly moist, but does not object to a sunny position if moist. Neither of them make a large root, and increase from divisions is very tedious, although both are long lived if left alone in the right conditions.

POLYGONUM *amplexicaule*

POLYGONUM *bistorta superbum*

POLYGONUM *affine* 'Donald Lowndes'

POTENTILLA ○

POTENTILLA 'Gibson's Scarlet'

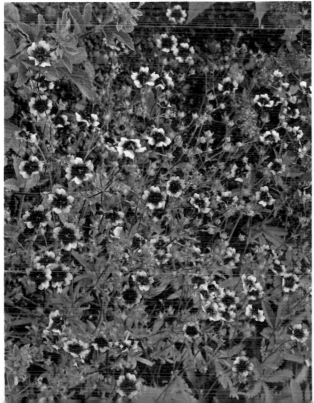

POTENTILLA 'Firedance'

POTENTILLA 'Glory of Nancy'

These have many good points and deserve to be grown more widely, for they will grow in just ordinary soil and will flower for a long time. P. *'Glory of Nancy'* is one of several with quite large flowers above pretty strawberry type leaves, in varying shades from green to silvery. This variety flowering June to August has grey-green leaves and the branching stems would be almost 2 feet if erect, but I prefer not to stake these taller ones any more than those dwarfer. They are not untidy in habit and look so much more natural. P. *argyrophylla atrosanguinea* has silver leaves and bright red flowers, May to July at 18 inches, but P. *'Yellow Queen'*, also silver, May-June flowering, is barely 12 inches. The intense blood red of P. *'Flamenco'* is outstanding, and it grows robustly to 2 feet for June-July, with P. *'Gibson's Scarlet'* a more prostrate variety which flowers from June to September. P. *'Mons. Rouillard'* is large flowered crimson, blotched orange whilst P. *'Wm. Rollisson'* is bright flame orange, 18 inches high. P. *'Firedance'* has smaller flowers in greater profusion of suffused orange, salmon and red colours at 15 inches, and P. *warreni* is an erect yellow flowered species for 2 feet., both with a long flowering season. Potentillas are easy to divide either in autumn or spring, and only P. warreni is best from seed. They are very colourful and very easy plants.

POTERIUM ○

PRIMULA

Primulas fall roughly into two categories—those that need moisture rather than shade, and those for which shade is a pre-requisite. P. *rosea* 'Delight' has no objection to sun, provided soil does not become dry and it makes a brilliant display in April-May, with flowers coming before the leaves. It makes a good companion for the 'Drumstick' Primula, P. *denticulata* which has lavender, blue, white or pink rounded heads at much the same time but is a little taller at 12-15 inches. There are scores of other Primulas for moist positions, as well as for shade, where if soil is humus rich, dampness is less important. Amongst these 'Woodlanders' is the all too little known P. *sieboldii*. These form shallow rooting mats and bear open heads of flowers in April-May. P. 'Geisha Girl' is a fine pink variety, and P. 'Snowflakes' is undoubtedly the best white. They like leafy soil and can be increased by division in spring, and it helps to give a light coverage of peat or leaf mould during the October-February period, when they are completely dormant.

POTERIUM *obtusum*

PRIMULA *rosea* 'Delight'

P. *obtusum*, this a another easy plant, for sunny positions and any soil. The roots are tough and spread slowly, and the stems, up to 2½ feet rise up to carry obtusely angled fluffy pink pokers, from June to August, and the leaves are fingered, glaucous of hue. There is a white form, and a taller white one, autumn flowering, in P. *canadensis*. P. *sitchense* (syn, Sanguisorba rubra) is more showy, producing lofty branching spikes of rosy red in the June-August period to 4-5 feet. This has a good habit, making large but compact plants and as with other species they can, with considerable effort, be divided in spring.

PRIMULA ○ ◐ ●

PRIMULA *sieboldii* 'Geisha Girl'

P. *vulgaris,* the well loved Primrose is
the progenitor of many hybrids which
are more adaptable than other Primulas. The best known of these is
P. *'Wanda'* with its purple-red flowers,
but there are many others in a variety
of colours from white to pink, through
to purple and red, and blue, as well as
those nearer to the original light
yellow. All these are best divided in
autumn.

PRIMULA *vulgaris*

This is the opposite view to that on p.40, taken in early summer and before bright colours outweigh the greens.

PRUNELLA ○

These are extremely easy to grow and though they do not have a long flowering period they make quite a show with their stumpy 12 inches spikes in June-July. All are mat forming plants with no deep roots, and all can be easily divided at any time when not in bud and flower. P. *'Loveliness'* covers three varieties, white, pink and lilac. There is a deeper pink species with dark green leaves named P. *webbiana*, and one with indented foliage and blue purple flowers called P. *incisa*, both flowering between June and August at 12 inches tall or less.

PRUNELLA 'Loveliness'

PYRETHRUM ○

PYRETHRUM *singles*

PYRETHRUM *doubles*

These were once grown in quantity for cutting, but stocks generally have dwindled. With their brightly coloured daisy type flowers in red, pink and white—both double and single, they are very decorative hardy plants whether or not used for cutting. They need very well drained soil with a preference for lime, and the somewhat carrotty foliage gives them a fresh appearance, whilst the very fibrous roots makes them easy to divide. This is best done in early Spring or in July after flowering. Good single varieties are P. 'E. M. Robinson', clear pink, P. 'Marjorie Robinson' deeper pink, P. 'Brenda' cerise, and

P. 'Evenglow', salmon orange, with a white sometimes available. Double flowered varieties are usually somewhat less vigorous. A good pink is P. 'Madeleine', with P. 'White Madeleine' also, and P. 'Carl Vogt' as another white. P. 'Progression' is a deeper pink and though double reds are scarce, there are a few such as P. 'J. N. Twerdy' and P. 'Lord Roseberry' in existence Singles grow to about 2½-3 feet and doubles usually a little shorter. Staking may be needed where grown in confined spaces and this should take the form of short pea sticks, inserted in early May, before the buds become heavy.

PULMONARIA ◗ ●

These are amongst the easiest shade loving plants and make a brave show from March to May. In moist soil shade is less necessary, and they are perfectly hardy and reliable, best divided in autumn where plants have become very old and unthrifty. One of the earliest and brightest is P. *angustifolia azurea*, with sprays of brilliant blue only 10 inches high, followed by the 8 inches P. *'Munstead Blue'*. P. *saccharata* *'Pink Dawn'* is a little taller and has quite large leaves which become heavily mottled with a near white variegation, giving rise to the name 'Spotted Dog'. This applies to others with the epithet P. *saccharata picta*, but there is P. *saccharata* *'Bowles Red'*, which though it has reddish flowers of the usual bell shape, is a rather coarse growing plant.

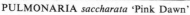

PULMONARIA *saccharata* 'Pink Dawn'

PULMONARIA *angustifolia azurea*

RANUNCULUS ○ ◑

RANUNCULUS *gramineus*

RANUNCULUS *aconitifolius plenus*

The wild Buttercup, R. *bulbosus* has several relations of good garden value and no weedy propensities either from seed or spread. Most of them prefer moist rather than dry soil, but R. *gramineus* is not fussy, preferring good drainage. The leaves are grassy and glaucous and from May to July send up erectly branching stems to 15 inches of glistening yellow cups. R. *acris plenus* is taller, with small but perfectly formed double flowers to 2 feet in June July. R. *bulbosus specious plenus* is a very refined dwarf Buttercup, with a rich green base foliage on a compact hummock. Flowers are fully double, 1½ inches across, slightly tinged green. R. *aconitifolius plenus* is the choicest of them all, needing rich moist soil and making a truly magnificent display May to July, with its countless little white buttons, in perfect double formation. This charming plant is also known as 'Fair Maids of Kent' and it takes a year or two for plants to become large, through the spread and height are about equal at 2 feet when happily settled. Division in autumn or early spring.

RANUNCULUS
bulbosus speciosus plenus

RHEUM ○

The ornamental species of Rhubarb are well worth growing though one of them needs ample space. R. *alexandrae* has leaves of modest size—rounded and smooth, and a compact rootstock.   In May come stems carrying curious but charming papery yellow bracts on spikes up to 3 feet tall, which stay effective for several weeks.   Ordinary good garden soil suits this unusual plant, as it does the more massive but imposing R. *palmatum*.   One should go for either the *rubrum* or *atrosanguineum* forms, since these are deep pinkish red when their 6 feet spikes open out in late spring.   The first leaves too are brightly coloured, from early April till flowering time—pink—red—purple, but after flowering, fading to green takes place.   These Rheums have such a wide spread when leaves develop that an established plant needs a 4-5 feet diameter spacing.   Division of Rheums is best in autumn or very early spring.

RHEUM *alexandrae*

RODGERSIA ◑ ●

These are handsome plants for both foliage and flower, but need moisture and some shade or shelter from strong winds which can spoil their beauty.   The plants are hardy enough, growing from slowly expanding surface rooting crowns to become quite large after a few years, but not difficult to divide.   R. *pinnata superba* is outstanding for its purplish tinged five fingered leaves, which make a canopy 2-2½ feet tall, above which come spikes of deep pink flowers in June-July.   There is also a bronzy leaved form, but most Rodgersias have large green leaves and creamy white plumes.   Other good species, apart from R. *pinnata* itself, are R. *podophylla* and R. *aesculifolia*, with a flat umbrella leaved species in R. *tabularis* which is dwarfer. All Rodgersias respond to a mulch in spring.

RODGERSIA *pinnata superba*

RUDBECKIA

RUDBECKIA *deamii*

For long flowering and general reliability the Rudbeckias rank highly for adding brightness in the garden in late summer and autumn, even though all are in shades of yellow. R. *deamii* will flower in great profusion from late July into October with its black centred rayed flowers. The height is 2-2½ feet, a little taller than the deeper yellow R. 'Goldsturm', which in good soil will flower for an even longer period. These supercede the old R. *speciosa* and there are taller, grey leaved species in R. *subtomentosa* and R. *mollis*, which grow 3-4 feet flowering July-September. The foregoing Rudbeckias are mat forming in the sense that they do not have a deep, compact root system, but a more shallow rooting outward spread. Nearly all such plants are of a hungry and thirsty disposition and when plants have been down for about 3 years, covering a much wider space, they may show some deterioration in the centre of the plant with less foliage and fewer flowers. The remedy is to apply some fertilised soil in that centre or to take up and replant using only the outer, more vigorous growth. R. 'Goldquelle' is outstanding for its erect bushy habit, well clothed with deep green leaves, and set with fine double chrome yellow flowers from early August into October. The height is little more than 3 feet, and a far tidier plant than the tall, floppy R. 'Golden Glow'. The best tall variety is single flowered R. 'Autumn Sun', but even this will reach 5 feet or more. All these Rudbeckias will divide in early spring and will flower for longer in good soil, not too dry, than where starved. See under Echinacea for what is still sometimes called R. purpurea—the 'Purple Cone Flower'.

RUDBECKIA 'Goldquelle'

SALVIA ○ ◑

SALVIA *superba (virgata nemerosa)*

To some people Salvia means the red bedding varieties, but others are perfectly hardy and S. *superba* and its varieties are amongst the finest of all hardy perennials. The type grows bushily to 3-4 feet with a long succession of violet purple spikes, from June to August and even longer if cut back. This applies to the 2½ feet S. *'Lubeca'* also, with a somewhat similar colour habit, as is the 1½ foot S. *'East Friesland'*. S. *'May Night'* grows about the same height, but the violet blue spikes begin in May and keep on for weeks. All these Salvias are easy to grow in ordinary soil, with good drainage. This is important and though all these are robust, long lived plants with no fads, they do dislike soggy conditions during winter months and when old especially, a rot may set in and losses may occur, if the spot is too damp. All have soft, slightly greyish leaves with a distinctive aroma. Division is best in spring, but young plants are quite safe in autumn. Another Salvia worth mentioning is S. *haematodes*. This has stiffly erect spikes of light lavender blue flowers in June, lasting on for many weeks and for a dry sunny place, the heavily silvered, woolly leaves of S. *argentea* are attractive even if the 2 feet sprays of white flowers are not very spectacular. Generally speaking Salvias prefer dry to wet places, but there is one S. *uliginosa*, which delights in damp soil. It forms matted growth below ground and sends up a profusion of slender stems to about 5 feet, tipped with short spikes of sky blue flowers. It can however be faulted on two counts. One is that it does not begin until well into September and though showy in a sunny warm autumn, it nearly always needs staking and in cold districts a covering of litter over winter as well. More erect and to a large extent the deeper blue. S. *ambigens* is an unusual plant. It grows stiffly and well foliaged to 4 feet and the deep blue flowers in terminal spikes are quite attractive. This is a long lived plant, best in sun, and in cold districts best covered over in winter with leaves. Finally, the Meadow Sage, S. *pratense* is not without merit, for it has arching 2 feet spikes in shades of blue and pink for several weeks.

Where spring division of old plants is recommended it does not follow that nursery grown plants must be planted in spring. Unless otherwise stated, the vast majority of nursery grown plants are safe in autumn, but often *old* plants are less vigorous and therefore less safe to divide until new growth begins in spring.

SALVIA *superba* 'Lubeca'

SCABIOSA ○

SCABIOSA *graminifolia*

The best known perennial Scabious is of course the blue S. *caucasica*, which is so useful for floral decoration. A good many varieties have been raised and introduced and of these S. '*Clive Greaves*', unlike many, has stood the test of time, both for constitution and colour. There are deeper blues such as S. '*Moerheim Blue*' and paler ones as in S. '*Moonstone*' as well as two good whites in S. '*Miss Willmott*' and S. '*Bressingham White*'. All grow to 2½-3 feet flowering from June to September. If dead flowers are cut, or others used for indoor decoration, it lengthens the flowering period. These Scabiosa must have well drained soil and they like lime. They are best planted or divided in spring and losses may occur as plants become old and woody after 3-4 years. From seed, S. *caucasica* comes in variable shades. Where grown other than as single plants it is good practice to divide a third of ones stock every year, beginning when the original plants are not more than three years old. It is when dividing old stock that planting losses may be heavy, and by this means, one has always younger healthier plants to go at. If there is any menace at all from slugs, they will go for Scabiosa during the dormant season and one should use slug bait, sharp ashes or lime around the plants. Two excellent dwarf Scabiosa are the mauve blue S. *graminifolia* and its pink variation S. *graminifolia* '*Pinkushion*'. These have silvery grassy leaves, forming an attractive mound a few inches high and above come a profusion of 'pincushion' flowers on 10-12 inches stems from June till well into September. Given well drained soil, both these are reliable, easy to divide and long lived. The light yellow S. *ochroleuca* is attractive and long flowering, but grows to a rather floppy 2 feet and is not very long lived. There is a close relative which is deep red flowered—*Knautia macedonia* (formerly Scabiosa rumelica). If its habit is to sprawl somewhat, anyone who grows it will not complain because it covers the ground with greenery at about 18 inches and above this come a long succession of deep red pincushions 2-3 inches across which are a delight.

SCABIOSA *varieties*

SEDUM ○

SEDUM *rhodiola*

SEDUM *aizoon*

SEDUM *spectabile* 'Brilliant'

Though mostly associated with Rock Gardens, there are some excellent Sedums which deserve full marks amongst the dwarfer herbaceous plants. There are enough kinds to cover the whole season, for S. *rhodiola* flowers in spring. It has a fleshy root and tufty yellow flowers above blue-grey imbricated stems to make a neat clump effective for a long time though only 9 inches high. S. *heterodontum* is a fine but little known plant of similar habit with bronzy foliage and burnt orange coloured heads in April. S. *aizoon* is a summer flowering yellow, and the best form is the orange coloured S. *aizoon aurantiacum*, which grows to about 12 inches with a coppery tinge to the leaves. Also in July-August there is the brilliant 9 inches S. '*Ruby Glow*' with headed flowers above glaucous foliage. This theme is magnified when the large plate heads of pink above 'ice plant' foliage open in September in the S. *spectabile* varieties, such as S. '*Brilliant*'. These do not differ greatly in colour, and all are about 15-18 inches high, with the 9 inches diameter

SEDUM ○

heads glistening and attracting bees and butterflies. The ultimate is S. 'Autumn Joy' for this has even larger plate heads, on stems almost 2 feet tall. The colour is light pink at first and by October has changed to a salmon shade till in early November it fades to russet. This is one of the finest plants ever introduced.

All these Sedums are easy to grow and are dividable in spring when old.

SEDUM *spectabile* 'Autumn Joy'

SENECIO

SENECIO *przewalskii* 'The Rocket'

S. *przewalskii*, this species has been included here, because the change of name for certain Senecios to Ligularias is somewhat hazy in peoples minds, and common usage is an important factor to consider. Regardless of which classification is correct S. przewalskii for all its awkward name is a very good garden plant for not too dry a position. It sends up narrowly tapering 5 feet spikes in high summer, which stand stiffly erect, and the stems are close to black in colour. The flowers themselves are bright yellow and though small and of a somewhat ragged appearance, contrast strikingly with the stems and the deeply cut leaves. The basal leaves too, are deeply incised, and of a size to provide a basal mound of foliage. I once came across a variation of this plant for which no variation was on records at my disposal, and was advised to give it a cultivar name to distinguish it from the type. The name chosen S. 'The Rocket' signifies its habit in flower, of sending up colourful spikes, even brighter than the type, and they come a week or two later. The leaves are more rounded but no less handsome. Both these plants make a large but compact clump, though easy to divide in autumn or spring and they revel in rich or moist soil without being a nuisance. Such upstanding, spikey subject can contribute much to variety of form in a bed or border.

SIDALCEA ○ ◑

SIDALCEA 'Rose Queen'

These are graceful members of the Mallow family, and smallness of flowers is compensated by profusion and long flowering. They seldom make very large plants, and losses may sometimes occur if not cut back after flowering. This encourages new basal growth for over-wintering, but old plants can be divided in spring. They are not fussy as to soil. S. 'Rose Queen' is one of the older varieties, reliably perennial, growing to 4 feet and flowering from June to late August. S. 'William Smith' is distinctive for its warm salmon pink shading and S. 'Croftway Red' is the deepest pink—nearest to red. Both these grow to about 3 feet but S. 'Rev. Page Roberts' and S. 'Elsie Heugh' are light satiny pink, with slender 4 feet spikes. S. 'Wensleydale' is of similar habit, with sizeable rosy red flowers and S. 'Loveliness' is a shell pink only 2½ feet high. Sidalceas along with other Mallow type flowers, prefer soil not too rich or damp. For many years I had been looking out for some dwarfer Sidalceas than those already in existence, because spike forming subjects are so helpful in obtaining a pleasing arrangement amongst the more round or flat headed kinds. With this in mind, Percy Piper, who has reared most of the Bressingham introductions, succeeded and three were selected in the 2-2½ feet range, all having a good habit in very attractive pink shades. I named them S. 'Oberon', S. 'Puck' and S. 'Titania', but having spent a few years in working up a sufficient stock to offer, they then showed some resentment at such intensive propagation. This appeared to be the only reason why, in 1965 we had over 1,000 plants of each, by 1967 they had to be virtually withdrawn because they either made too little growth to give propagating material, or planting losses decimated stock.

SIDALCEA 'William Smith'

SOLIDAGO

SOLIDAGO 'Golden Gates'

The 'Golden Rods' have undergone a great change in recent years, with the taller, weedier kinds being ousted by the more discerning gardeners for those that are more compact and give a better show. S. *'Leraft'* was the first of this new race growing only 2½ feet tall and flowering in July-August. S. *'Golden Shower'* is another, slightly taller representative and in their varying shades of yellow, and shape of the plume, S. *'Golden Mosa'* S. *'Golden Gates'* and S. *'Lemore'*— a lemon yellow, can be well recommended. For something dwarfer S. *'Crown of Rays'* is leafy with prominently lateral spikes, only 2 feet high, and S. *'Peter Pan'* of similar habit 3½ feet. Amongst the real dwarfs, late flowering, S. *'Laurin'* makes a wide foliage and flower spread, but S. *'Queenie'* and S. *'Golden Thumb'* form little bushes barely 12 inches high. Both have somewhat golden green leaves and deep yellow flowers, making them ideal for frontal positions, where compactness counts. Solidagos appreciate good soil, and divisions of old plants is an easy matter in spring.

SOLIDAGO 'Golden Shower'

STACHYS ○

STACHYS *densiflorum*

STACHYS *lanata*

There is nothing difficult about any of the Stachys, and there are one or two lesser known kinds which should be more widely known. S. *lanata* is not one of these, for as 'Donkeys Ears' it is seen in many a garden, popular for its rapid surface spread of felted silver leaves and 20 inches sprays of small pink flowers. These are not very attractive and in the variety S. *'Silver Carpet'* there are none, and the plant lives up to its name as a first class ground covering subject, capable of growing between shrubs, withstanding drought and can be planted at almost any time. S. *byzantinus* is even more vigorous, with larger leaves. S. *macrantha* makes neat 2 feet bushes with bright lilac pink flowers of good size in June and July and the variety S. *macrantha robusta* is earlier and stronger growing. S. *spicata robusta* is very erect and spikey, flowering bright pink to 2 feet and S. *spicata densiflorum* has tightly packed spikes at 18 inches. These are two excellent long flowering but little known plants, clumpy but compact; and there is a charming dwarf white S. *nivea* (stricta alba) which grows only 8 inches flowering a long time. All these grow in ordinary soil and can be divided. This genus has come in for nomenclature re-classification in recent years, with the inevitable result that there is conflict between common usage and correctness. Quite often, the only grounds for a change of name by the botanical authorities is that of the first recorded name of a plant being given priority. As a principle this is fair enough, but when a plant has been known under a certain name for a century or more, it is asking rather a lot of ordinary gardeners to make the change, when botanic names are difficult enough to memorise anyway. In this case it was decided that plants under the generic name of Betonica ought to be transferred under Stachys. Only the botanical experts can give the technical reason, and ordinary gardeners along with nurserymen can but follow suit, or no compromise is possible and sometimes they dig in their toes and stick to the best known name. Amongst the above S. *macrantha* and S. *spicata* were Betonicas until a few years ago, as Betonica grandiflora and spicata respectively, and may still be occasionally listed under these names.

SYMPHYTUM ⦿

SYMPHYTUM *rubrum*

S. *rubrum*. Most of the 'Comfreys' are coarse growing, but S. rubrum is outstanding not only for being compact, but for its red flowers which continue for a very long time. These come on sprays up to 12 inches tall, from early June, with a background of deep green foliage. Roots are fleshy, not difficult to divide and the one important requisite is moistish soil, with a preference for some shade, though it is by no means a bog plant.

This is a subject I was lucky enough to rescue from obscurity and some plantsmen did not know that it existed. At first I placed it in deep shade but it did not thrive until I moved it into partial shade and moister soil, since when it has never looked back. It flowers for a much longer period than S. *caucasicum*. This In its way is quite pretty, for it has blue flowers on 2 feet stems during June and July. This and the rather coarse 2½ feet S. *peregrinum* with blue flowers that fade to pink, are best suited for the 'wild garden'.

THALICTRUM

THALICTRUM *dipterocarpum*

The illustration is of only one of several kinds of which can add great charm to the garden. T. *diptercarpum* likes rich soil and from a comparatively small plant sends up much branched stems to 5 feet which need supporting. It lasts in flower from July to September as does the dwarfer, choicer T. *'Hewitt's Double'*, which prefers some shade as well as rich moist soil. Several Thalictrums carry large heads of yellow, fluffy flowers and are stronger and more erect. T. *angustifolium* is one of the best, flowering at 5 feet in June and July. T. *aquilegifolium 'Thundercloud'* has purplish fluffy heads on 3-4 feet stems, from May to July. These last three are happy in ordinary soil and open positions, though T. *rocquebrunianum* likes it rich and it is worth applying an occasional mulch to see the blue-green stems grow strongly to 4 feet carrying its charming lavender lilac flowers in June and July. All Thalictrums have delicately pretty leaves and all but the first two mentioned are easy to divide in spring.

TIARELLA ◑ ●

T. *cordifolia* is the aptly named 'Foam Flower'. It needs a shady place and leafy or peaty lime free soil. In this it will spread quickly with pretty leaves of a somewhat golden hue, and in May-June is covered with 6 inches sprays of foamy white flowers. Division is best in autumn or very early spring. T. *wherryi* is taller and has very little surface spread. Instead it makes a low mound of golden green, prettily zoned leaves of ivy shape and carries a long succesion of 12 inches spikes of creamy-white. This is one of the parents of *Heucherella* '*Bridget Bloom*' but is a very worthy plant in its own right for a cool shady place. T. *polyphylla* is more adaptable, making leafy evergreen hummocks bearing 10 inches sprays of flowers like tiny pearls, from June to August.

TIARELLA *cordifolia*

VERBASCUM ○

V. '*C. L. Adams*' is one of the best of the perennial 'Mulleins' with its very effective 4 feet spikes of deep yellow flowers from June to August. The leaves are quite large and the roots are fangy and from these root cuttings, increase can be made. All Verbascums like an open sunny position and well drained but otherwise ordinary soil—poor rather than rich. There are a good many kinds and other reliable yellows are V. *chaixii* and V. *thapsiforme*. V. '*Gainsborough*' is a charming light yellow, 3 feet tall, with silvery grey leaves and V. *hartleyi* has a suffusion of biscuit yellow and plum purple flowers on 5 feet spikes. V. '*Pink Domino*' is dark leaved, spikes being 3 feet tall for the same June-August period. There is a white in V. '*Mont Blanc*' and multicoloured flowers in V. '*Cotswold Gem*' and V. '*Cotswold Queen*', both 3 feet. A small flowered, but neat growing V. '*Golden Bush*' is outstanding, for it is only 2 feet high and lasts in flower longer than any other. Verbascums can be planted in either autumn or spring but will not divide.

VERBASCUM C.L. Adams'

TRADESCANTIA ○ ◑

TRADESCANTIA 'Purewell Giant'
               'Osprey'
               'Isis'

TRADESCANTIA 'Purple Dome'

T. *virginiana*, Though not by any means choice, the Tradescantias have at least two good points in their favour. One is that they flower for a long time and the other is on the score of reliability and hardiness. On the debit side, it must be said that they take on a rather tatty appearance after being in flower for a couple of months and that they do not stay erect unaided when in damp or rich soil. They begin flowering in June when about a 12 inches high, but by August will be 18 inches or more, with their three petalled flowers (hence the name 'Trinity Flower') continuing to open on clustered heads. The foliage is rushy and glaucous green, and the plants are quite rooty, though not difficult to divide. T. *'Purewell Giant'*, carmine purple, T. *'Osprey'*, pure white and T. *'Isis'*, deep blue, are, with T. *'Purple Dome'* a good selection from the varieties in cultivation.

TROLLIUS ○ ◑

These 'Globe Flowers' are moisture lovers, but any good garden soil which does not dry out in summer will grow them successfully. The roots are densely fibrous, and the crowns will open out on old plants for division, carrying a portion of the roots. They can be divided and planted in very early spring, or better still in early autumn. Flower buds begin to show long before they actually open in late May, and until late June, they make a luminous display in shades of yellow. T. *europaeus superbus* along with T. *'Earliest of All'*, are the first to flower, the latter being a little deeper in colour and a little taller at 2½ feet. Height is no advantage, and varies somewhat with moisture. T. *'Goldquelle'* has very large mid-yellow flowers, but T. *'Fireglobe'* is a shade deeper than T. *'Orange Princess'*. For a pale yellow, T. *'Canary Bird'* is excellent and as with all these Trollius the rich green foliage is fully complementary. T. *ledebouri* has less foliage and the flowers are less globular, but such a variety of T. *ledebouri 'Imperial Orange'* is worthy of a place not only because it flowers after

TROLLIUS 'Fireglobe'

TROLLIUS 'Goldquelle'

others of the europaeus type have finished, but because of its rich deep colour, enhanced by prominent stamens. This grows to 3 feet flowering from mid-June to early August. These are amongst the plants which benefit from a mulch of compost; peat, or even organic fertiliser can be mixed in beforehand—about a cupful to a bushel, or it can be sprinkled around the plants by itself, prior to applying a mulch about an inch thick. This is an easy alternative to replanting when plants tend to deteriorate with age and has a revitalising effect. In the case of Trollius it can be applied immediately after flowering (or in autumn) and it will not only conserve moisture but often induce a second crop.

VERONICA ○ ◑

This genus varies all the way from a filmy surface mat in some cases to plants growing 5 or 6 feet. Generally speaking they are easy to grow, and this applies to varieties of V. *teucrium*. V. *'Crater Lake Blue'* makes a brilliant show in June-July, barely 12 inches high, and V. *'Shirley Blue'* is only 6-8 inches. V. *'Blue Fountain'* is taller, up to 2 feet, all flowering at about the same time. One of the earliest is V. *gentianoides* which has light blue spikes to 2 feet in April-May, from bright green mats, but V. *spicata incana* is grey leaved with 1 foot spikes of violet flowers— less free than the slightly taller V. *'Saraband'* and the rather untidy grey leaved V. *'Wendy'*. These flower from June to August and need well drained soil. V. *longifolia 'Foersters Blue'* is a deep colour, the spikes coming on bushy green leaved plants 2½ feet high. Much taller, later, and lighter in colour is V. *exultata*. In August and September this has 4 feet spikes on which saw-edged green leaves hang. The most imposing tall Veronica is the white flowered V. *virginia alba*. The spikes run to 5 feet tapering gracefully with whorled leaves, and stems strong enough to resist any gale. There is a blue and a pale pink V. *virginica*, but V. *alba* remains effective for longer during late summer. Apart from V. *incana* and those in its group best planted in spring, Veronicas can be planted at any time when dormant and are generally long lived and trouble free.

VERONICA *incana*

VERONICA *teucrium* 'Crater Lake Blue'

VERONICA *virginica alba*

VINCA

VINCA *minor*

Several ground covering plants have been included, since the need for them exist, especially where little else will grow. The 'Periwinkles' or Vincas are outstanding in this respect for they can survive in the most inhospitable of places and remain evergreen, although it must be said that they grow best and flower best in half shade where not bone dry. Vincas come in two groups, V. *minor* and V. *major*, and as one would expect the former are smaller in growth. They have also the widest range of colour even if freedom to flower is not one of the strong points of Vincas generally. The freest is the bright blue V.'*Bowles*

Variety' and V. *atropurpurea* is a plum purple shade, of more rapid spread, as has the white V. *alba*.
The variegated leaved are naturally brighter in foliage effect, and both the silvery V. *argentea* and the golden V. *aurea* are worth having. V. *major* has leaves twice as large as V. *minor*, but is no quicker to spread. These make less of a carpet, but both the green type and the bright golden-green of V. *major variegata* are useful and attractive. Old Vincas tear apart quite easily, but are not so easy to plant safely as young pot grown plants.

VINCA *minor* 'Bowles Variety'

VINCA *minor atropurpurea*

YUCCA ○

YUCCA *filamentosa*

Y. *filamentosa.* Some Yuccas are said to flower only once in seven years, but Y. filamentosa seldom misses a year, given a sunny place and well drained soil, once it has become established. This is a subject for isolation, where its symmetry can be appreciated, and when in flower during July and August it is an imposing sight with its ivory bells on spikes 4 or 5 feet high. The sharp pointed leaves of this species has small drooping loose threads along the edges, and being evergreen, the woody stem lengthens with age. Plants will however produce suckers from the roots which in time mature to make a single plant become a group. When planting in autumn, a collar of litter should be placed around for protection over the first winter, but once established it can take care of itself.

ZANTEDESCHIA ☉

To see 'Arum Lilies' growing naturally in the garden may come as a surprise. No one can deny their effectiveness and given a moist soil and a sunny situation they will flower from July till well into autumn. Provided they are given a protective covering during November they will come through again in spring and increase in size year after year. Although this Arum Lily is the least hardy of any subject mentioned in this book, the *'Crowborough Variety'* is by far the most reliable for outdoor cultivation. Along with other subjects in need of winter protection it is fully worthy of inclusion for the sake of its outstanding qualities because protection is such a simple matter. From experience I have found that these tender subjects, which are fully herbaceous and not shrubby are more likely to come through wintry conditions left in situ than if dug up and placed under cover in autumn. They rely on below ground vitality to survive, as do all plants and root disturbance in autumn can be fatal. Winter covering can be of leaves, straw, or even peat or soil provided a piece of thick polythene sheeting or sack can be placed over or wrapped round first. Zantedeschia and some others do not die down until frost comes, and it is after this elimination of any foliage that final adjustments should be made to whatever is used as covering. The basic need is to keep roots and crowns from freezing, and this means that the soil between and around plants must be adequately covered. A 6-9 inches depth of leaves or straw will ensure that no frost penetrates through to the soil even in the coldest districts.

ZANTEDESCHIA *aethiopica* 'Crowborough'

Other subjects in need of protection are listed below, but except in very cold districts those marked x would only need it in the first year after planting, as resistance to frost in these cases increases with age and establishment. In all cases winter covering should be removed as soon as new growth begins in spring. Such timing will vary from late February or early March in southern and western districts to early April in more northerly and hilly areas.

x Agapanthus
x Alstroemeria.
x Anemone japonica.

Cautleya robusta.
Centaurea pulchra major.

x Crinum.
x Cynara.

Kniphofia, erecta.
x Kniphofia - other kinds.

x Lavatera olbia.

Montbretia.

x Nerine.
x Penstemon hartwegii varieties.
x Perowskia.

x Roscoea.
x Ruta.

Saxifraga fortunei and varieties.
Schizostylis.

Tovara virginiana variegata.
x Tricyrtis.

x Yucca.

Zantedeschia.

Yucca filamentosa is the most reliable to flower. Its tall spikes dwarf the curiously flowered *Roscoea beesiana* in front.

GRASSES

Ornamental grasses are becoming much more popular nowadays and despite their lack of colour in flower, some make an excellent foil to other plants, whilst others with attractive foliage, are worth growing for this alone. Those varieties mentioned below are only a few of those available from specialist catalogues.

FESTUCA *glauca*

AVENA *candida*

AVENA

A. *candida* is a simpler name than *Helictotrichon* which is said to be correct. It is a blue-grey evergreen hummocky grass, with narrow foliage up to 18 inches or so. Above this in early summer there are hazy plumes of flowers, but these are best cut off when faded.

CORTADERIA

C. *argentea* is the well known, majestic 'Pampas Grass', which is best in isolation or against a background of evergreen. It is not safe to plant this until new spring growth begins in April. Even so, division of old plants is risky and losses may occur.

FESTUCA

F. *ovina glauca* will transplant at almost any time and keeps its colour throughout the year. Flowers are of little value, and are best cut off as they fade. At only 6-8 inches high this is a neat grass for edging, or to plant *en masse* on a bank or anywhere as ground cover. F. *'Eskia'* is similar in habit but of a rich deep green colour.

HAKONECHLORA

H. *macro-alba aurea variegata*, this unwieldy name stands for one of the most charming dwarf variegated grasses. It is newly introduced from Japan but is quite hardy and has but a modest spread, preferring a good light soil, not too dry. Height is 9-10 inches and leaves die back between November and March, when now growth begins.

HAKONECHLORA *macro-alba aurea variegata*

CORTADERIA *argentea*

LASIOGROSTIS *splendens*

MISCANTHUS *japonicus* 'Silver Fern'

MOLINIA *caerulea variegata*

LASIOGROSTIS

L. *splendens*, has handsome 3-4 feet plumes of creamy buff in June-July on wiry stems. The plant is fairly compact, green leaved, is easy to divide in spring and it is not fussy as to soil.

MISCANTHUS

All the Miscanthus are reliable and though all have attractive foliage, M. 'Silver Fern' is the only one that flowers freely. In late summer and autumn the plumes rise to 6 feet or so, and make a real focal point in the garden. The leaves, as with the type, M. *japonicus*, have a whitish midriff, but in M. *japonicus zebrinus* they are striped or banded horizontally, with alternating yellow and green. M. *japonicus variegatus* is the finest tall variegated green I know, with the fine upstanding habit of the genus, and brightly variegated from April to November.
M. *japonicus gracillimus* is narrow leaved, and as graceful as the name implies. M. *sacchariflorus* is a giant, running up to 8 feet with broad, drooping leaves which afford not only a wind-break, but rustling shade as well. All Miscanthus have a slow, but steady spread. They can be left alone for years, but are best planted in spring.

MOLINIA

M. *caerulea variegata* is charming in both leaf and flower. It is not evergreen, but foliage is colourful from April to November, whilst during later summer, the flower sprays provide a hazy overtone to the foliage. Spring planting is best and good soil, not dry, is preferred. M. *altissima* grows reedily to 4 or 5 feet, pretty all summer but in autumn biscuit yellow and very effective.

CONCLUSION

It is my belief that in terms of value for money and effort, Hardy Perennials exceed any other section of decorative gardening. It is nearly fifty years ago that I first became attracted to them and my main working life has been devoted to them. It is on this experience that the above testament of belief is based. It is also from this experience that the text of this book has been written. But experience covers more than knowledge of plants. It has to include ones failures, the amount of work, some pleasant, some tedious, which has been entailed. For many years, I had to confine work to the production of Hardy Perennials for sale, working up a mainly wholesale business. It was not until the mid 1950's that I was able to make a real garden devoted almost entirely to Perennials. By 1962 it covered five acres and contained about 5,000 different species and varieties. Amongst the thousands of visitors who come to see this garden every year are a few who find it a little disheartening. Its all very well, they say, but I have the setting and the scope for Island Beds, and really 'going to town' on Perennials, but they have only a small garden patch, and they find even this difficult to keep tidy and colourful. My answer to them is that, no matter how small or even inhospitable, there are kinds of plants that will grow there, if a careful choice is made. They cannot expect something for nothing. It takes thinking time as well as effort to get the best out of any garden space. The axiom that what you get from life is measured by what is put into it, applies also to gardening. But it must be said that some forms of gardening are more demanding than others. Annual bedding is probably the costliest in this respect, having to replant beds twice a year to obtain a display from spring till autumn. A few people have gone in entirely for shrubs or ground coverers but are seldom pleased with the result which even if labour saving, provides little by way of interest. Even a garden entirely of lawn, needs frequent regular attention and gives nothing but a sward of greenery. But Hardy Perennials are a two way investment. The initial cost relative to shrubs or ground coverers, is very low. Yet having made ordinary preparations and a careful choice of Hardy Perennials, one has a variety of plants that will not only live on from year to year, providing not only colour and beauty, but interest as well. It is the latter that inspires and stimulates, that makes the little effort required by way of maintenance, infinitely worth while. This is the reason why, speaking from experience, my belief in the value of Hardy Perennials has increased with the passage of time.

INDEX